D1234376

Bruce E. Massis, MA, MLS

The Practical
Library Manager

Pre-publication
REVIEW . . .

"**B**ruce Massis, author of *The Practical Library Manager,* has written a useful and, as the title implies, practical book for library managers new to the field.

This book will help new library directors accept and manage change in order to transform the organization and meet the needs of internal and external customers. Massis believes that cheaper and faster technology will keep customers away from the library if library services do not adapt to the changing needs of customers.

The book focuses on staff training and provides several tools to help the new library director. Massis provides various useful lists throughout the text, bringing together information from a variety of places. The new manager will find it handy to have all of this information in one place.

The aspiring library manager should dip into this book from time to time to address practical library management problems in the rapidly changing library environment."

Samual F. Morrison, MLS
Director, Broward County Library,
Ft. Lauderdale, FL

The Practical
Library Manager

HAWORTH Cataloging & Classification
Ruth C. Carter, Senior Editor

New, Recent, and Forthcoming Titles:

Technicial Services: A Quarter Century of Change: A Look to the Future by Linda C. Smith and Ruth C. Carter

Cataloging and Classification for Library Technicians, Second Edition by Mary Liu Kao

Introduction to Technical Services for Library Technicians by Mary Liu Kao

Puzzles and Essays from "The Exchange": Tricky Reference Questions by Charles R. Anderson

The Practical Library Manager by Bruce E. Massis

The Practical Library Manager

Bruce E. Massis, MA, MLS

The Haworth Information Press®
An Imprint of The Haworth Press, Inc.
New York • London • Oxford

Published by

The Haworth Information Press®, an imprint of The Haworth Press, Inc., 10 Alice Street, Binghamton, NY 13904-1580.

PUBLISHER'S NOTE
Due to the ever-changing nature of the Internet, Web site names and addresses, though verified to the best of the publisher's ability, should not be accepted as accurate without independent verification.

Cover design by Lora Wiggins.

Library of Congress Cataloging-in-Publication Data

Massis, Bruce E.
   The practical library manager / Bruce E. Massis
      p. cm.
   Includes bibliographical references and index.
   ISBN 0-7890-1765-2 (alk. paper)—ISBN 0-7890-1766-0 (pbk.)
   1. Library administration. 2. Library personnel management. 3. Library employees—In-service training. 4. Public libraries—Administration. I. Title.

Z678 .M35 2002
025.1—dc21
                                                                                          2002068604

Dedicated to the memory of Johannes Daugbjerg,
my dear friend and mentor.

.

ABOUT THE AUTHOR

Bruce E. Massis, BS, MLS, MA, has served the library profession as a respected library manager for more than two decades. He presently serves as Associate Director of the Southeast Florida Library Information Network. Previously, he was the founding Director of the JGB Cassette Recording Library International, Division Manager of the Brooklyn Public Library's Central Library, and Director of the Hoboken Public Library. Mr. Massis has served in official positions within the International Federation of Library Associations and has been active in the American Library Association, the New York Library Association, the Long Island Library Association, the New Jersey Library Association, and the American Society for Training and Development.

Mr. Massis' professional publications include *Interlibrary Loan of Alternative Format Materials* (Haworth), *Serving Print Disabled Library Patrons,* and *Library Service for the Blind and Physically Handicapped: An International Approach.*

CONTENTS

Acknowledgments

I would like to thank the following friends and mentors who have helped me to better comprehend scholarship, management, and a profession I continue to respect and remain excited by, even after offering more than two decades of service to it: Richard Barsam, Georgette Clark, Hardy Franklin, Martín Gomez, John F. Heimerdinger, E. J. Josey, Susan Kacen, Brian Kenney, Allan Leach, Dina Reilly, Jack Salzman, Susanne Seidelin, Beatrice Christensen-Skold, Tom Sloan, Nic J. Snyman, Ken Stanley, Winnie Vitzansky, Robert White, and, of course, Traci Aquara.

Introduction

For the decades leading up to the new millennium, the phrase "public service" clearly appeared to be misapplied to the American workforce. It frequently appeared that those in general public service positions provided a poor quality of service matched only by a general abhorrence of the public they were "sworn" to serve. One did not have to attempt anything more exotic than a visit to the local Department of Motor Vehicles to recognize that the only thing many public service employees despised more than service was the public.

Jobs in the public sector were generally assumed to offer little more than the promise of lifelong employment for layabouts and slackers. Work at a public service institution would either get done or not, and it mattered little to the bottom line because, in effect, there was no bottom line. Municipal tax dollars would be appropriated for a laundry list of public services, including libraries, which would simply roll on, year after year, fulfilling their mandate, such as it was, and very little else.

Parents guiding their children into this area of employment would often counsel them to accept a position in a public agency only because, regardless of qualification or performance, it was "safe," "comfortable," and lifelong employment. Awaiting them at the end of three decades in such an environment would be a solid benefits package providing a comfortable retirement. After dealing with the public, they believed they had spent their time in the pits and deserved a rest.

To be fair, many individuals working in public service agencies, especially libraries, did indeed deserve the gift of a dignified withdrawal from public service. To their credit, a certain percentage of employees who entered the system and endured their quarter of a century or longer conquered the bureaucratic jungle while on the job, at least those with the courage, compassion, and wisdom to do so. Such individuals made a difference, and over the course of time the system slowly evolved into one where a more humanistic and educated approach prevailed.

After many years of shoddy service and ever-diminishing public expectations, an apathetic haze settled over the public. Due to a phenomenon known throughout the world of charitable agencies as the "halo effect," where the public is willing to accept whatever small tokens of service are doled out by an agency, the public was willing to accept this situation and generally kept silent. Those who balked at something they did not like were often viewed as crackpots and were punished by the offended agency with even worse service, if not outright exile.

It could also be a hard, cruel world for library "patrons" as well. Because libraries are supported with tax dollars, they could vote a municipal library's budget in or out, but where else would they go for their information needs? There was no alternative. Books were expensive. Microfilm, microfiche, and back issues of journals were not readily available on one's home shelves. There was, of course, no Internet. So, there was little choice. Good service or bad, the library doors would remain open, and tiny dollops of service were doled out as the institution saw fit.

The fiefdom walls that enclosed each public service agency were so impregnable, and in many ways the agencies were so intolerant and unbending, that they believed totally in their own position. But as technology evolved and the nation's need for information became critical, things were forced to change.

Patrons demanded better, more responsive, and more able public services. Libraries changed their terminology. Patrons were being renamed "customers," and libraries became responsible for every single line item in their budget, thus creating the effect of a bottom line. They accepted the corporate sensibility of their own "return on investment" (ROI). Simply stated, this is the measurable benefit derived from the library's investment in its one product, service delivery. No longer was it acceptable for libraries to simply fulfill their mission. As in any successful corporation, a library had to design its business plan for the coming fiscal year with an eye to creating measurable outcomes for all of its services, including the staff delivering those services.

Cheaper, faster technology in the hands of the public provided them with a means of actually bypassing the public library to access information. While attendance figures showed that people were not staying home yet, they unmistakably would in the not-too-distant future. In the university environment, younger, more technologically savvy students who had essentially grown up using the new technologies noticeably began to favor electronic access to print materials, rather than the print materials themselves. There was recognition, in both the public and academic sectors, that library managers could no longer conduct business as usual. Thus, the move toward a more open, smart system was essential. Library service would have to be much more attuned to its clientele and directly responsive to its customers' needs.

The halo effect all but disappeared in the eyes of this sharper, tougher, more demanding customer. In the new millennium, the expectation that all public agencies should provide the best, most professionally competent customer service has risen enormously. For a library to survive these changes, it is clear that, while the image of the cold, hard-hearted bureaucracy remains a fixed image in some people's minds, the new approach to friendly, knowledgeable, considerate customer service must replace what came before.

Today, the most successful libraries in the country are those which regularly address and administer to the direct needs of both external and internal customers. Libraries that have adopted change as the norm are models of excellence for all libraries so that they may continue to evolve into the cutting-edge agencies they must become.

However, it takes more than technology to change the working relationship between the institution and its customer. To successfully negotiate the rough waters of change, the guiding force behind this change must include a strong and respectful partnership between the library manager and the library staff.

Whenever financial gurus are queried about the importance of the Federal Reserve and its relationship to the stock market and the economy, the response is usually something like, "The Fed is the whole ball of wax. As the Fed goes, so go the markets and, in a larger sense, the entire economy." Likewise, in terms of asking about the relationship of the staff to the library, the response should also be, "The staff is the whole ball of wax. As the staff goes, so goes the library." Continuous training and regard for the staff should remain uppermost in the mind of the library manager. Without the staff, there is no service. The doors cannot remain open. Therefore, this book concentrates on two basic concepts: (1) that the staff is a library manager's most important asset and (2) that the varied meanings of the word "practical," more than any other, can serve the library manager well in a climate of change. The two concepts intersect in the recognition by the library manager that practical management of the library depends on the practical management of the library staff.

Therefore, this book is primarily designed for library managers new to the field. Much of what is written here can assist the fledgling manager in creating an environment of trust, teamwork, and respect. Finally, as valid as the practical hints are, so too are the bibliographies and appendixes included herein. This book should be used as a tool with which the library manager can successfully manage the climate of change that is so pervasive in libraries today.

A primary thread running through this book is a sense of encouragement: encouragement to the library manager to accept change and work along with the staff to assist in their acceptance of change in order to transform the organization in which they all work. The reader will encounter the word "change" both directly and in a number of guises, and by the end it is hoped that he or she will be transformed as well.

Although many of the examples may appear to relate best to public libraries, apart from nuances in governing bodies and their politics, laws, and regulations (e.g., a municipality holding the purse strings of a public library budget as opposed to the college or university administration serving as the governing body of the campus library), I maintain that basic, practical library management applies to any library, whether public, private, or academic.

Chapter 1

The Challenge of Staffing

The greatest challenge facing library managers in the new millennium is, in my opinion, planning, implementing, and evaluating an ongoing viable training program for library staff. A number of important questions arise regarding this issue.

- Are recent library school graduates receiving adequate instruction in library management issues to prepare them to become effective library managers?
- Do working library managers have to be trained, or retrained, to lead their staffs through an extended period of inevitable change?
- How must the library be properly staffed to provide the most appropriate and responsive customer service within an expanding technological environment?
- What is the most effective leadership technique a library manager can rely on to encourage the staff to participate in a climate of rapid change?
- Who will perform the staff training?
- How and where, in an environment usually plagued with extremely limited space, will the staff receive training?

A library can install the most sophisticated and technologically advanced equipment available, but if the staff is not properly trained or does not wish to be trained, then that equipment becomes merely decorative. Increased and ever-changing technology in the library has led to two conclusions: (1) technology has placed the library squarely in the center of the information revolution, and (2) it has certainly changed the way in which the staff does its job.

Library staff must be equipped with an entire mental tool kit for negotiating their way through the tasks facing them each day in their work. They must possess a multitude of abilities such as the capacity to offer knowledge of the latest search engines and the means by which to search the Web with the greatest fluency, and even be able to design and maintain a library Web site. They must also have infinite patience and the training to work with a public whose expectations regarding quality customer service, in general, and electronic information, in particular, are the most demanding in history, a public whose expectations often far exceed a library's resources.

When the library "customer" arrives at the reference desk, he or she fully expects to receive the answer to a query not only immediately, but usually online. It is at this moment that expectations sometimes exceed reality. Much to the customer's apparent dismay, the reference librarian must sometimes satisfy his or her information need with a print resource. The librarian hands the customer a book, not a printout, and the look of horror and disbelief on the customer's face is palpable. The fact that he or she must actually paw through a volume of printed text bound by two covers scares the pants off him or her, and the inevitable next question is, "Isn't this available online?"

Well, the truth is, not everything is available online. Not by a long shot. But it remains the librarian's job to educate the public and guide them to the proper resource, whether it is available in print or online. Convincing the public that they still must occasionally receive their information from a text is becoming a more difficult task, as the public believes something entirely different.

This is as accurate in academe as in the public libraries. More often than not, hordes of students will arrive at the college or university reference desk clamoring to log on to the library's computers because they were given assignments that must be accomplished without the use of print resources. Even some literary or historical assignments, those which were once *only* accomplished through using print resources, are now often assigned as computer exercises.

While there is certainly an enormous amount of electronic material, (we are presently dealing with a trillion-page Web), the truth is, an equal amount of information remains available in print. Any knowledgeable and experienced reference librarian can quite often find the answer to a reference query faster with a print source than one online. Also, if a limited number of public workstations are available in the library, a customer will have to wait until a terminal becomes available. That could mean waiting hours in one of the larger public or university libraries. Yet many would still rather do that than use the print resource. There is the very real image of a computer waiting area set directly in the middle of the reference room, or elsewhere within public view, the chairs filled with customers patiently awaiting their turn at the workstation. The area is completely surrounded by bookshelves filled to bursting, and still most customers sit and wait, never going to the shelf to select something to read while they do so.

For the library manager, budget, of course, often has an impact on whether the reference librarian can find the answer to a particular query in print or online. As the balance between the purchase of print titles and electronic titles becomes more precarious, the budget planning team must decide how these funds are to be expended. But it remains the task of the collection development team to decide on the specific materials to be purchased and in what format. The expenses of all formats are reaching such astronomical heights that the library manager must inevitably decide what is to be jettisoned and what to retain.

For example, does a library purchase a business directory that is used marginally at the cost of say, $1,000, rather than a business database that will cost several hundred dollars more, but can be updated quarterly for several hundred additional dollars? While the print version must be purchased in its entirety the following year at an even higher cost, the electronic version can often be purchased in "modules" that include the most recent updates that will not appear in the print version until the next year. It is an item that is only used sporadically, but those who use it like the print version and are comfortable with it. How does the library manager decide what to buy when budgets are relatively flat or slightly increased, but the cost of reference materials may be rising as much as 10 percent or more each year?

The difficult decision that has to be made by the collection development team may well be based simply on cost and what will offer the most potential usage. Juggling the budget in a situation of ever-increasing costs and tightening budgets has always been a challenge to the library manager. While libraries cannot purchase everything (after all, more than 60,000 titles are published in print every year), they must weigh every dollar spent against the usage those materials receive. Specialty items can be bought, but they are more and more a luxury in which most libraries cannot afford to indulge. This too becomes the task of today's library manager: being responsible not only for the purchase of the appropriate materials to fill out a library's collections, but to purchase them in the most appropriate format.

Assuming that someday everything will be online, the information world will, perhaps, be a much simpler place in which to navigate. However, until that splendid (or, to some, horrifying) moment arrives, library managers must be able to use their expertise to steer the information ship with a crew who may or may not be outfitted with the navigational tools with which to learn to steer themselves.

To begin at the graduate school level in answering one of the questions posed at the start of this chapter, one must take a look at the library schools and ask if they have caught up to the realities of what their students will face when they begin work as professionals in the field upon graduation. In examining the curricula of a sampling of the fifty or so library schools in the United States, one sees a noticeable lack of management training courses. A number of programs offer a single course, labeled either "The Management of Information Environments," or "Organization and Management," or "Administration and Management," or finally just "Library Administration." While the curriculum is filled with courses on the history of the book, cataloging, subject specialties, technology, and hundreds of resource courses, very few schools offer more than a cursory glance at library management to their students, many of whom will go on to become directors. Are library managers to learn the about complexities foisted upon them by technology and their own customers, armed with no more than, perhaps, a single course in library management? Such a lack of proper training for our library school students shortchanges them and does not properly equip them for what they will face in the field as potential administrators.

In this writer's opinion, the best library training program in the country in terms of its responsiveness to the needs of the potential library director is offered by the school of Library and Information Science at the University of Wisconsin, Milwaukee. Not only are an impressive number of management courses included in the curriculum, but they are actually broken down into type of library, be it public, academic, or special. Equally important are courses dealing with library issues most often encountered by the modern public library director, including "Evaluation of Library Services," "Information Policy," "Legal Issues," and "Intellectual Freedom."

Theirs is a program that has looked at the real world of library management and recognizes its complexities. The library school student who is fortunate enough to attend this library school, or one with an equal level of management training, will indeed take away all the tools necessary to begin a career as a budding library manager. Other academic institutions may look to this model and seek to duplicate it if the profession is to offer more basic management training to our potential library managers. It is not fair to send them into the field devoid of the proper tools. They should not be expected to learn all their skills while on the job.

This brings us to the second question posed at the beginning of this chapter. Potential library managers should not be blamed for not receiving the appropriate amount of management training. Perhaps their library school did not offer much in this area. Perhaps they were not fortunate enough to work for a library system that offered basic and/or refresher courses in management training for professional staff. There is often a great deal of discussion in libraries regarding an administration's intent to promote from within, but often the reality is that an institution seeks employees from outside the regular staff in order to obtain a "fresh" look at the issues of the day. Perhaps a new perspective is needed to solve a particular crisis. Perhaps not. With a strong, coordinated effort supported by the institution, the in-house staff may be urged to think "out of the box." Also, administrations seem to overlook the reasons why they hired their staff in the first place, and the staff's attributes may be dormant or simply not respected enough to be expressed. It is then up to the administration to offer the onboard staff the opportunities to join the team and make a difference. If they require further training to do so, then they should be offered that chance.

Staff retention is a crucial issue facing the profession due to a surplus of jobs and the variability of professional starting salaries. Therefore, library administrations must take a hard look at the necessity of establishing or enhancing their continuing education and training programs in order to maintain and thus promote staff members from within. Library managers must seek to build a real team environment within the institution. Administrations must learn to listen to their staff. The staff must, in turn, avail themselves of this training if they are to have designs on management positions in the future.

This text places a great deal of emphasis on staff training. But, of course, the initial training period for professionals occurs in library school. Library managers might consider a partnership with a library school in which the library school serves as a professional incubator. Librarians being trained for the field today have their choice when it comes to job selection. Jobs in the field have not always been so plentiful. But the explosion of technology along with the accessibility of jobs for librarians *outside* libraries have opened the opportunities for recent graduates even further. The kind of on-campus recruitment regularly practiced by corporations may serve as a useful model for our short-staffed libraries to replicate. A partnership with a library school in the area may serve the library manager by providing new staff educated in the most modern technological and other library practices. The library manager will find the list of ALA-accredited library schools in Appendix A a useful tool to serve as the primary contact in this partnering.

An additional potential staffing opportunity not to be overlooked by the library manager is the hiring of paraprofessional staff. There are a number of paraprofessional training programs that offer an educational opportunity to those who wish to work in the library, but who may not be ready to commit themselves to a full undergraduate, then graduate program in library science. The library manager might also partner with one of these programs in order to have the program placement office consider his or her institution first when placing graduates of these programs. Support staff hired from these programs will come equipped with desired training, so the environment of the library will not seem alien to them. In such cases, less basic orientation will be necessary.

Within ALA, the Support Staff Interest Round Table (SSIRT) was established with the intention to support staff members working in libraries around the nation who do not hold the MLS but whose work certainly supports that done by librarians. SSIRT states that its "membership is composed of proactive library personnel who are essential to the cultural, educational, and economic life of our nation's libraries. We represent academic, public, school, corporate and special libraries. We have an interest in, and activity with, other ALA groups and interrelate with all library personnel."[1] The SSIRT home page and its allied links, which include SSIRT national resource listings and other information, may be consulted to learn more about the means by which library managers may contact SSIRT. Also, the Council on Library/Media Technicians (COLT) for the appropriate region of the country may be contacted at <http://library.vcr.edu/ COLT/executive.html#chapters> to broker a partnership that could result in additional trained staff. The following Web sites will prove useful for the library manager in contacting the appropriate library support staff group:

<http://www.ala.org/ssirt/>
<http://www.lib.rochester.edu/ssp/orgs>

Chapter 2

The Impact of Technology
on the Library Manager

It is hardly an understatement to suggest that no single issue has more transformed the world of libraries and information delivery services than the impact of technology. Coincidentally, in recent years, more ink has been spilled in the cause of the Internet and its related subjects of filtering and censorship than any other single issue appearing in the library literature. A veritable library of material has been written on the subject. There is little I could add to the arguments. The library manager may consult the bibliography for a selection of books and articles on the subject. However, it would be of great benefit for the library manager to read the literature on a weekly basis to keep up on the subject. Professional publications such as *Library Journal, American Libraries, Library Administration and Management,* and *Library Hotline* are required reading both in print and, if available, in their digital formats.

In the last decade, libraries have moved out of the slow lane of the information delivery industry directly onto the fast track. Because the Internet has caused such a transformation, the library manager must be aware of certain terminology regarding electronic access and the statutes being created that impact service delivery of information, both positively and negatively. Examples of the most common statutory developments follow. However, it is imperative that the library manager frequently consult the ALA website for the latest news regarding the pertinent legislation being monitored by the ALA Washington office (www.ala.org/washoff). Especially relevant are the following legislative initiatives:

- *Children's Internet Protection Act* (CIPA)—CIPA was enacted on December 15, 2000. It went into effect on April 20, 2001. These laws place restrictions on the use of funding that is available through the Library Services and Technology Act, Title III of the Elementary and Secondary Education Act, and on the Universal Service discount program known as the E-rate (Public Law 106-554). These restrictions take the form of requirements for Internet safety policies and technology which blocks or filters certain material from being accessed through the Internet. The ALA is in the process of challenging this statute. The latest updates may be found at: <http://www.ala.org/cipa>.

- *Child Online Protection Act* (COPA)—COPA would have made it a federal crime to use the World Wide Web to communicate "for commercial purposes" material considered "harmful to minors." In a unanimous decision issued on June 23, 2000, the Third Circuit Court of Appeals struck down the Child Online Protection Act as unconstitutional. Libraries are safe from this legislation for the moment.

- *Digital Millennium Copyright Act* (DMCA)—The Digital Millennium Copyright Act was passed in the last days of the 105th Congress in 1998. The Act seeks a balance between protection for copyright holders and reasonable access for users to copyrighted works. In order to learn what the DMCA means to the library manager, analysis written by experts in the field may be found at the ALA Web site. These include:

  —Interpretation of Section 108(a)(3) of the Copyright Act, 17 U.S.C. § 108(a)(3), as amended in DMCA (August 18, 1999)

  —What the DMCA and the Copyright Term Extension Act Mean to the Library Community: Primer by Arnold Lutzker (March 8, 1999)

  —Library Preservation: Changes Incorporated in The Digital Millenium Copyright Act of 1998, P.L. 105-304 (November 12, 1998)

  —Digital Millennium Copyright Act: Analysis by Jonathan Band, Morrison and Foerster LLP (October 20, 1998)

- *E-Rate*—Under the E-Rate program, libraries may be eligible for extensive telecommunications discounts annually. An extensive application process must be followed for all applications. For more information, go to: <http://www.ala.org/washoff/e-rate.html>.

- *Fair Use of Copyright*—Simply stated, "fair use" provisions of the copyright law allow limited copying or distribution of published works without the author's permission in some cases. Examples of fair use of copyrighted materials include quotation of excerpts in a review or critique or copying a small part of a work by a teacher or student to illustrate a lesson. Libraries are authorized to exercise special rights in addition to fair use. These rights are described in Section 108 of the copyright law and include the following:

—Archiving lost, stolen, damaged, or deteriorating works
—Making copies for library patrons
—Making copies for other libraries' patrons (interlibrary loan)

• *Library Services and Technology Act* (LSTA)—The Library Services and Technology Act was passed and became P.L. 104-208 on September 30, 1996. LSTA built on the strengths of previous federal library programs, but included some major advantages and differences. While it retained the state-based approach from previous legislation, it sharpened the focus to two key priorities for libraries—information access through technology and information empowerment through special services. It also relocated library program offices from the Department of Education to a new Institute of Museum and Library Services (IMLS). Libraries may apply for LSTA grants within the guidelines of the two areas annually through their state libraries. The library manager should consult his or her state library for further information regarding applications, deadlines, reporting, etc.

• *"The Uniform Computer Information Transactions Act* (UCITA)— is a proposed state contract law developed to regulate transactions in intangible goods such as computer software, online databases, and other information products in digital form. UCITA was originally intended to be a revision to the Uniform Commercial Code (UCC), which has been adopted in almost all of the states and territories of the United States and which ensures consistent rules governing contract law from state to state. Because the two legal bodies charged with drafting changes to the UCC failed to agree on a draft, the proposed statute is being introduced in each state as a stand-alone addition to the state's legal codes. Publishers and large software producers are the primary supporters of UCITA. Libraries, consumer protection groups, and a number of businesses have been among those opposing the enactment of UCITA as it has been introduced in several states starting in Fall 1999."[1] The latest ALA opposition to UCITA was voiced at hearings in 2001 before the UCITA Standby Drafting Committee. For more information on UCITA, go to: <www.ala.org/washoff/ucita>.

Thanks to these legislative initiatives and the Internet itself, never before have libraries and library-related issues been so prominent in the headlines as in recent years. Library managers are spending much more time responding to the press, local legislators, and potential funding agencies in order to present an image of the knowledgeable, forward-thinking manager who is aware of the issues and their ramifications for the library.

The twin issues of open access and filtering have certainly made the profession a much more vibrant and exciting one in which to participate. The debate is being fought by the ALA and the ACLU every day, and with the strong support of the membership, the ALA has been gifted with professionals who are unwilling to give in to pressure. The ALA remains a professional organization assisting its membership through the increasingly complicated world created by the transformation of the print world to the digital one.

In the arena of new technology, public expectation is often fueled by the media. Since the media is quick to report on the latest, hottest "big thing" in technology, the public hears so much about it (whatever *it* is) that they expect to encounter it immediately. They want to walk into their public library and find the fastest, most comprehensive machines and the most knowledgeable staff trained in the use of these machines. In the era of rising expectations, the public has little patience for old, slow technology or ill-trained library staff. This expectation has kept the libraries on their toes in terms of regular upgrading of their own technology in order to keep in step with the public.

The public has demanded that libraries provide them with the most current, cutting-edge technology to serve their information needs. Customers regularly remind the library staff that their taxes support library services. This is both true and somewhat inaccurate in that while a certain amount of tax dollars directly support the public library, the public would be surprised at what a small amount of their taxes it is.

Because the Internet has changed the world in so short a time and in so many ways, for some library managers there is still a great deal to learn. For others, this change has become second nature. It is important for library managers to concentrate their efforts on several of the issues relevant to managing technology in a practical manner in the new millenium:

- Offer continuous technology training for library staff
- Design a strong, supportive Internet policy
- Develop an intelligent collection development policy as it relates to electronic resources
- Create a balance between electronic and print products (do not abandon print in favor of electronic access yet)
- Keep up on the latest trends in technology

Access to the Internet has become an issue of "damned if we do and damned if we don't" regarding filtering. A library can be hauled into court for filtering and, equally, for not filtering, especially regarding computers located in the children's area of the library. The library must at least have a policy in place so that when confronted with the issue, from one side or the other, the library can formulate an appropriate and consistent response. As guardians of the First Amendment, librarians have always been proud to provide open access to information. In terms of control, libraries have always had collection development policies to guide them in the materials selection process. Quite simply, certain materials are appropriate for the library and certain materials are not. Does such a statement fly in the face of the First Amendment? A staunch First Amendment rights activist would probably say yes, citing the argument that what is appropriate for one person may not be appropriate for another. Each individual's definition of what is appropriate and what is not appropriate varies with the individual. However, quite often library computer workstations with access to the Internet are out in the open and offer no privacy for the user or for those casually lingering in the area. Therefore, the definition of what or what is not appropriate must be defined by the library itself, through its policy-making body, the board of trustees. Although the policy decided upon may not offer any real protection against a lawsuit, at least the library is exhibiting a sense of understanding of the issue by taking responsibility for creating an Internet policy.

A good place to start, if the library manager has not yet done so, is to see what others have done. The ALA Office of Intellectual Freedom has been instrumental in leading the charge regarding appropriate responses to the most sensitive of censorship issues. The library manager must become familiar with the materials available through this office, including its frequent Web alerts on pressing areas of concern. Simply log onto <www.ala.org/oif> and register for these alerts. To remain current on these issues is paramount during this age of mounting calls for censorship and filtering. (A Web bibliography concentrating on censorship and filtering issues has been included in the bibliography.)

By writing and standing by a library's clearly defined Internet policy, the staff can have something substantial to fall back on in times of public inquiry. If, however, the policy supports open access, where the responsibility for Internet use is placed squarely on the user (or when it comes to children, the parents of the user), the library opens the door to public abuse of the technology and even potential abuse of the staff.

Politicians regularly employ open access on library computers as an excuse to wage war on the "liberal" policies of a library. In certain communities this is a hot-button issue. There is no argument that the issue receives a great deal of publicity and libraries must spend an inordinate amount of time defending their policies during these challenges. There is even real cause for fear that filtering of library computers will be tied to federal, state, or even local funding and that all-important public funding could be lost if libraries do not succumb to a filtering mandate.

So, clearly, or unclearly, the lines have been drawn. The library manager must not only be able to stand tall and defend the library's policies when tested but must also position himself or herself in a position of support for the staff, who must stand squarely on the front lines of service carrying out the policies set down by the library.

An excellent resource for the library manager to research on this issue is <www.filteringinfo.org>. The site is updated regularly, and since the issue itself is one that requires the library manager to stay informed with the latest news, the site should be bookmarked for frequent reference.

Chapter 3

Building Core Competencies
for Library Staff

The concept of building core competencies for library staff has been an issue of debate for quite some time. The concept of core competency has actually been in existence, in one form or another, since the turn of the twentieth century. According to Alain J. Godbout in his article, "Managing Core Competencies: The Impact of Knowledge Management on Human Resources Practices in Leading Edge Organizations," "The term was reintroduced into management jargon (in 1989) . . . in the context of globalization of markets and rapid technological change."[1]

Over the years, there have been numerous attempts at defining specific responses to the construction of a sweeping set of competencies for library staff. How "can" one define core competencies? Perhaps core competencies are the proficiency and knowledge necessary for an employee to perform his or her required duties and provide defined services. Equally important, core competencies must serve to synthesize one's skills and knowledge and define one's performance requirements.

While the term "core competencies" has become overused in both the profit and nonprofit sectors, the core competencies themselves have been much more difficult to construct. Criteria created to define these competencies are often denigrated or maligned by management and/or staff for being too narrow or too broad. Further, if the environment is unionized, each set of competencies, while written by management, must often be scrutinized and approved by the union prior to its acceptance and implementation.

As technology continues to dominate the workplace, competencies that appear appropriate today are often obsolete tomorrow. Still, there must be a means by which a criterion of evaluation may be defined so that managers and staff alike are held accountable to a measurable standard.

The development of core competencies must also be designed so that the definitions respond to change in the workplace as readily as change occurs. If change is indeed to become the standard operating procedure in the library, it is necessary to periodically review and, if necessary, update these competencies. The jobs of most library staff have changed quite dramatically of late, from limiting and fixed to fluid and adaptive, from having a constricted focus to a much more extensive one. Fortunately, a number of universities and libraries have already addressed the core competency issue from a variety of perspectives:

- The *entire* staff
- A *segment* of the staff
- *All* aspects of staff skills
- *Specific* sets of staff skills

A cursory look at several examples may serve to assist the library manager whose intent is to create core competencies.

Example I: Core Competencies for the Entire Staff: University of California, Riverside (UCR)

The UCR study of core competencies was written in response to what was perceived as their "need for an increasingly flexible workforce, able to assume new responsibility quickly based on changing conditions . . ."[2] The study team succeeded in classifying thirteen core competencies under which nearly 150 descriptive skills were also identified:

1. *Creativity:* applies new ways of thinking; creates new ideas
2. *Vision:* understands the context of the organization within the outside world; is aware of the organization's critical success factors; anticipates and influences the future
3. *Influence:* having an impact on others; convincing them to perform certain activities; garners respect; inspiring them to work toward organizational objectives
4. *Entrepreneurship:* understands customers; builds organizational credibility; develops new revenue sources

5. *Organizational Design and Development:* organizes for success; understands how to facilitate functional needs and structure to achieve strategic plans
6. *Building Teamwork:* cooperates to achieve common goals; values and encourages diversity of opinions; creates synergies across the work group
7. *Communication:* clear expression of ideas and thoughts as well as active and empathetic listening
8. *Understanding Self and Others:* healthy, trusting interpersonal relating; accurate self-assessment; understands that people process information differently; takes initiative to build relationships; understands cultural differences
9. *Development of People:* enhances one's own ability and the ability of others to contribute
10. *Performance Management:* motivates; delegates; clarity and specificity of expectations
11. *Program/Process Management:* resource utilization and maximization; time, financial, and human resource management
12. *Staffing:* identifies and defines needs; attracts appropriate candidates; determines fit; selects the most qualified
13. *Compliance/Ethics:* personal compass composed of clear principles and the flexibility to balance between literal adherence to rules and the use of policy as a guide.[3]

The application of core competencies is as important as their construction. The UCR model suggests four succinct objectives with the aim of ensuring they are achieved. Therefore, the core competencies identified in this model must meet the following four objectives:

1. All staff and leadership are equally clear about content, key activities, and required skills of all roles.
2. All staff and leadership are equally clear about the training and development it will take to do the job.
3. A dialogue will take place between leadership and staff about objectives, targets, priorities, and expected talents and competency levels.
4. A focus is created on activities that are valued and support the organization's achievement of goals and objectives.[4]

The effectiveness of sensibly designed core competencies for library staff must be inexorably linked to concrete outcomes and measurable goals. One of the merits of the UCR study is that it does so, and while it is specifically related to their own environment, it may be adapted to many university or public libraries.

What if the library wishes to concentrate its efforts on creating core competencies only for a single group of staff (e.g., the librarians)? We have already mentioned the model for creating competencies for the entire staff. The following two examples differ from the former in that the focus is on a specific group of staff.

Example IIa: Core Competencies for Specific Staff:
The New Jersey Library Association

According to the document produced by The New Jersey Library Association, "NJLA Core Competencies for Librarians," the following outcomes are sought:

- To stimulate service excellence
- To renew enthusiasm for the profession among librarians
- To be used to develop job descriptions and evaluation tools for professional positions
- To assist in planning a continuing staff development program
- To be used in the development of policies, particularly as these policies relate to the organization and staffing of libraries
- To guide students who, while attending graduate library school, appraise faculty who are involved in the development of curricula of the continuously changing needs of the profession
- To educate communities, governing bodies, and funding agencies about the importance of the skills and knowledge of professional librarians[5]

The reader will notice that the issue of technology is not specifically addressed in expected outcomes of this model, although it is listed under Professional Competencies. The NJLA document states, "Expertise with and willingness to use technology is underlying all areas in the field of librarianship today. These competencies underpin the delivery of services to all ages, all constituencies and for all types of libraries." [6]

This model is broken down into professional competencies and personal competencies as follows:

Professional Competencies

- Customer service
- Assessment
- Knowledge of information sources
- Resource management
- Technical skills
- Advocacy
- Collaboration
- Administration

Personal competencies

- Education
- Service commitment
- Flexibility
- Leadership
- Ethics
- Communication
- Self-motivation

(For a full explanation of all bullets, go to: <http://www.njla.org/statements/competencies.html>.)

A second example of competencies designed specifically for librarians comes from the California Library Association (CLA).

Example IIb: CLA Competencies for California Librarians in the Twenty-First Century

Much like its predecessor, this set of core competencies, adopted by librarians statewide, is broken down into professional and personal areas. This is a work in progress to be reviewed periodically "as the demands of the library profession in California change."[7] Particularly of note are their definitions of professional competencies and personal competencies:

Professional competencies relate to the librarian's skills and knowledge in the areas of information resources, information access, technology, management and research, and the ability to use these competencies as a basis for providing library and information services. Personal competencies represent a set of skills, attitudes and values which enable librarians to provide valuable and valued service, communicate well, survive in the new world of information, and focus on continued learning throughout their careers. These skills, attitudes and values can be acquired through education and experience the same as professional skills and knowledge.[8]

Although this language differs slightly from that in the previous model, the areas of concern are quite similar:

Professional Competencies

- Customer-centered
- Assessment
- Organizational skills
- Knowledge of information sources
- Information management
- Advocacy
- Collaboration
- Political awareness
- Administration

Personal Competencies

- Service commitment
- Flexibility
- Leadership
- Ethics
- Vision
- Communication
- Self-motivation

(For a full definition of each bullet, go to: <http://cla-net.org/pubs/Competencies.html>.)

Example III: Core Competencies Designed to Accommodate All Skills: The Tampa Bay Library Consortium (TBLC)

The TBLC has defined a series of core competencies in all general skill areas. This organization has offered an important set of suggested skill areas to be examined when designing an inclusive set of competencies. The design committee writes that although "common threads were examined and this list reflects competencies that should be developed in all library employees . . . libraries will further refine the individual items to suit their needs."[9]

A cursory look at the TBLC categorical breakdown reveals broad categories and within each are subcategories from which a more narrowly focused listing may be created. Competencies in this model fall into four distinct categories, each followed a number of specific areas of competence as follows:

Philosophical Competencies

1. The mission/role of the library
2. Relationships within the library
3. Relationship to other libraries (cooperation and resource sharing)
4. Relationship to the community
5. Professional ethics and values

Technology Competencies

1. Computer skills
2. Audiovisual
3. Information retrieval
4. Library's role

Professional Competencies

1. Education
2. Knowledge of information access
3. Knowledge of information scope
4. Customer service
5. Communication

6. Collaboration
7. Evaluation
8. Advocacy

Personal Competencies

1. Personal development
2. Self-motivation
3. Services
4. Flexibility
5. Interpersonal skills
6. Communication
7. Leadership
8. Problem solving
9. Resource management

Example IV: Core Competencies—Specific Skills: Oakland Public Library

One of the most comprehensive sets of core competencies yet produced for public library staff (in this case, focusing on technology) comes from the Oakland, California, Public Library (OPL). An excellent model for larger public library systems, this document may be used as an outline for others to follow in terms of its ability to fully define, at least as much as possible, a very specific set of skills necessary to negotiate a very specific set of organizational technology requirements.

The crux of this model is the definition of each and every job title in terms of the *technological expectations* for that job. Prior to delineating core competencies by job title, a checklist of skills that all staff should possess is suggested, including the following:

- Log automation system terminals on and off
- Access e-mail
- Operate photocopiers
- Operate telephone handsets properly
- Use fax machines
- Printer skills
- Basic computer skills (on/off, boot up, insert/remove floppy disk)

- Check automation system bulletin board
- Read automation system internal mail
- Navigate automation system menus
- Access automation system help screens
- Understand cables, power cords, on/off switches (basic cable management)

While we often accept "basic" technology (telephones, faxes, copiers, etc.) as ordinary, a significant number of individuals do not possess the requisite experience to navigate such devices. For these individuals, specific skills training must be made available for them to better perform their duties. Therefore, during the design phase of a comprehensive staff technology training program, the staff's inability to negotiate their way through even the most basic level of technology must be considered.

While Oakland Public Library has created a set of minimum competencies, they emphasize in the introduction to their report that "interested staff are encouraged to learn more than the minimum and may attend workshops on other skills. . . ."[10] (For a complete listing of all job titles for which core competencies have been created by the OPL, go to <http://www.oaklandlibrary.org/techcomp.htm>.)

In a profession where salaries remain consistently below parity with other professions, there must be other incentives to retain staff. One of the strongest supports for boosting salaries can be a set of comprehensive core competencies leading to an inclusive staff training program. There must be the ability for staff to move up in the organization. Without these opportunities, the incentive to remain in place is removed. Morale disintegrates, and individuals' ability to serve the public can be severely hampered.

A well-designed set of core competencies must serve to identify and support the training necessary to perform the skills associated with each job. Areas of training that have not yet been addressed may be designed so that skills learned may neatly fit into a particular core competency. While there may be similarities in the kinds of work done within each job title, there will undoubtedly be some differences in specific tasks that may be directly addressed by further training. So it follows that as fluid as the core competencies are, so must the staff training program be, especially where the primary duties to be accomplished are technology based. As written in a report by the

University of California at Riverside (UCR), "employees must constantly operate in a learning mode."[11]

Personnel at all levels should have a basic skill set to help them more effectively perform their jobs. If everyone in libraries builds a basic level of competencies, they can all more effectively communicate with each other and work together. Library managers must stress that individuals who do not bring up their skills can reduce the effectiveness of an entire department. It also must be emphasized to staff that even though core competencies may be in place, libraries will always welcome the efforts of individuals to take their skills beyond the core competencies. This is where the continuing education and training initiative becomes critical. As a measurable result of an established set of core competencies, a continuing education and training team must be established to work to develop or identify a training program that will help all staff to achieve skills that will offer them the opportunity to go beyond the basics.

A number of selected Web resources have been identified to assist the library manager in creating core competencies, which may be found in the bibliography.

Chapter 4

Challenges and Opportunities for Planning and Implementing a Training Program for Library Staff

Those who believe we are living through a mere period of change are missing the big picture. For change has, or should have, become the norm across the entire spectrum of library services. As the library world settles into this climate of change, one is led to two distinct conclusions: (1) that technology has placed the library squarely in the center of the information revolution, and (2) that a librarian's job has been fundamentally and irrevocably altered.

Librarians and information technologists must be equipped with an updated mental tool kit from which they can select the proper tool for the task. They must also demonstrate a proven ability to multitask if they are to successfully offer the highest quality public service. In the electronic arena, they must demonstrate their capacity to access a wide range of appropriate electronic resources during a reference interview. They must be competent to search the Web with the greatest fluency and even be graced with the aptitude to design a library's Web site. They must also possess infinite patience and humanity in order to work with a public whose expectations of quality customer service grow greater each day.

An important distinction between training and education is that education often stops after the transfer of knowledge is complete. While trainers and teachers strive for their students to learn and comprehend subject matter to acquire new knowledge, trainers are more concerned with how that knowledge can and will be applied in the work environment. Therefore training may be defined as the systematic acquisition of skills, rules, concepts, or attitudes that result in improved performance. Training must be continuous and ongoing so that the scope of staff's capabilities, learning, and experience becomes as extensive as possible. Every library's annual budget *must* contain a line item that incorporates staff training and, for as many staff as possible, mandatory attendance at professional meetings and conferences (which, in its own way, is another forum for training) if libraries are to attract, develop, retain, and promote knowledgeable and qualified staff.

THE CHALLENGES

In today's technology-rich library environment, training is a cross-functional activity that affects all staff. The library manager may be encouraged when staff are eager to incorporate technology and customer service enhancements into their daily work—both from an individual task perspective and from a need to best assist the customer. Although they may exhibit less enthusiasm when it comes time to update their customer service skills, staff must recognize that change in today's library requires supplements to these skills as well, and is equally important and essential. Also, prior to beginning a staff training program, the library manager must ensure that both solid logistical and philosophical supports are in place so that the program is successful.

Logistics Checklist

It is important for the library manager to work with trainers (or perhaps even be a trainer) to ensure that the logistical details are all in place prior to the start of training. A checklist of these details includes:

- Proper scheduling so that departments are not left short-handed while staff are out at training sessions.
- Supervisors must be notified when and for what duration of time their staff will be involved in the training session.
- The registration procedure (if there are a number of courses and a large staff) or direct assignment (if there are fewer courses and a small staff) must be done in a reasonable amount of time prior to training.
- Record keeping must be accurate so that staff may be placed in the appropriate course and know which ones may require prerequisites for the next level.

- Course curricula must be reviewed by the library manager for content and clarity.
- Space must be set aside for the training to occur.
- Equipment must be in the training location and must be in proper working order.
- The library manager must make certain that, after technology training is completed, the technology is in-house and ready for operation so that the staff's skills remain sharp upon their return to the job site.
- Written evaluations of the course must be designed by trainers and completed by staff so that administrators can review the effectiveness of each staff member.

Challenges That Can Undermine Training

A common challenge regarding the training of library staff is that they approach it with varying levels of confidence and ability. Therefore, it is up to the library manager to assess the needs of staff by surveying them and responding accordingly.

Other problem situations may arise during training and can undermine the value of the training experience. These may be addressed by the library manager, along with the trainers, prior to library staff's participation in the training, so that the credibility of the sessions is not eroded. Such problems might include the following:

- *Direct challenges to the training concept or the trainer's credibility:* The response to the former is to confirm that the concept has different degrees of value for different people in different situations but is still useful. To the latter, the response is to secure the perception of the participants that the trainer can deliver a useful training experience.
- *Little or no participation, or someone is dominating the discussion:* The response is to create a more dynamic, participative learning environment.
- *A staffer drifts off and is noncommunicative:* The response is to encourage the participant to focus on the concept being taught to the entire class.
- *Distracting side discussions in the training room:* The response is to create an atmosphere where it is understood that distrac-

tions that can threaten the success of the training program must be minimized.

- *A staffer asks a difficult question:* The response is for the trainer to provide the staffer (and the class) with an accurate and satisfying answer.

Challenges to Effectiveness

There are also number of challenges to the *effectiveness* of classroom training. A checklist of these would include the following:

- Do not overload staff with too much information.
- Offer mainly work-related exercises during the class.
- Staff must be able to see the instructor and/or classroom monitor.
- Each staff member must attend the correct level of training.
- Course materials and handouts should be available for staff to take back to the job site for reference purposes.
- Use hardware or software breakdowns as an additional learning challenge.

Challenges to Momentum

Equally critical is the challenge of maintaining momentum. It is critical for staff not to lose what they have learned. Therefore, when they return to the job site, these challenges, too, must be overcome.

- Staff must have access to a computer.
- Staff must have the proper computer software.
- Circulation system training must result in better, more comprehensive, direct customer service, and more timely and correct responses to customer problems.
- Staff must immediately apply what they have learned in their daily work.
- Learned customer service skills must be used every day, if not on the desk, perhaps with other staff.
- Staff must be encouraged and supported by management to overcome the tendency to drift backward into old habits.

- Staff must be encouraged to attend additional training sessions, mandated by the library manager, if necessary. Training must be considered a top priority.
- Staff may be encouraged to share what they have learned with other staff in order to keep it fresh in their minds and to create a sense of teamwork.
- Staff must be provided with bibliographies (in print and online) so they can continue individualized training upon returning to the job site.

THE OPPORTUNITIES

Training must afford the staff the opportunity to learn both core and specific skills. Core skills are those in which every staff member must prove his or her competency (e.g., Microsoft Office, automated circulation system, Windows operating system, Linux operating system, etc.). Specific skills are those that are crucial to an individual's job description and on which that individual's performance can be evaluated (e.g., subscription databases, internal and external searching skills, internal and external customer service techniques, etc.). The library manager must be able to work with the trainers to stress that training will not *add* new tasks to staff's daily work, but will *enhance* their ability to perform those tasks. The library manager also must be able to work with the trainers to make the training exercises as positive an experience for staff as possible.

The Opportunity to "Train the Trainer"

The library manager must identify staff members who might be able to become trainers themselves. The concept of "training the trainer" is one of the most utilized training models in participatory management. It is the comprehensive practice of training enthusiastic individuals and those who possess a strong commitment to staff and who are the unique combination of teacher, psychologist, and guru to train others. It is a fortunate library manager who has in-house staff blessed with the ability, after receiving such training, to respond to the need for trainers.

Continuous staff training offered by in-house talent can result in an exceedingly professional staff, well-versed in the nuances of their daily routines. It also serves to relieve the library manager of the time and cost of bringing in outside trainers. One of the values of having such individuals onboard is that precise training modules, specific to the job site, may be designed by those most familiar with the staff's needs. Besides attending regular train-the-trainer sessions themselves to update their own skills, the in-house trainers may also avail themselves of a number of written and online sources.

The "Distance Training" Opportunity

As the expansion of cable continues and eventually reaches a saturation that includes every neighborhood in every state, the option of distance training via the Internet clearly becomes an option. The concept of distance learning has been in place for several years. The growing development and use of "streaming video" will result in much better delivery of signal, thus offering greater opportunity for learning. Also, as this technology becomes commonplace and the price of the equipment decreases, many more organizations and individuals will be able to access available offerings. The feasibility of this method of information delivery can be investigated as plans for the library's or consortium's training plan are developed.

If the library manager can inspire and lead the library staff in such a manner that they approach a training program with an upbeat and proactive attitude, staff will recognize that what they are learning will make them better at what they were hired to accomplish, thus furthering the mission of the institution. Therefore, it is imperative that staff view every challenge as an opportunity to learn and to strengthen their abilities, in order to make them a more viable commodity in the information delivery marketplace for the institutions who employ them.

Retreats and Conferences

Even after technology rollouts and upgrades have become the normal state of affairs in a library, the manner in which the electronic environment has affected the institution will continue to be ignored by a certain percentage of the workforce. This unwillingness to embrace change can be attributed not only to line staff but to some library managers as well. Herein lies the greatest challenge in an environment of change, for it is the managers who must lead the charge into the brave new world. It is they who must assume responsibility to keep the organization moving forward.

It is also the responsibility of the library manager (and the management team, if the manager has established such a team) to continually, or at the very least annually, refresh his or her own leadership skills so there remains a high level of executive accountability for the organization's progress. One means of achieving success in reaching the goals set forth by the library is to organize a retreat. A professional facilitator familiar with guiding an institution through its growing pains can be an essential element in maintaining a strong, goal-oriented, mission-driven organization.

Seeking out a professional facilitator to spend a day or two each year to work with an organization's executive staff is a task that must not be undertaken lightly. The library must find one who has been recommended, perhaps by respected colleagues or by national reputation. This individual may not even be one who has worked specifically with libraries and librarians. This is not as important as engaging a facilitator who possesses the experience of working with an organization whose size and values closely match that of the library staff with whom they will work.

A number of individuals who work in the library world tend to think that we do so in a vacuum, that no one outside that world could possibly understand the "unique" work situation and the unusual work structure, terminology, difficulties, etc. in which libraries operate. But every industry has its own manner of working, its own distinctive language and currency with which it operates.

Library managers must understand that, in terms of management techniques and abilities, there is almost nothing they do that is particularly uncommon among managers in any industry. Therefore, the utilization of a corporate management facilitator to lead a workshop focusing on the issues important to the library manager and his or her team must be considered when selecting an appropriate person for the job.

There are managers who, because they believe the myth of the library industry's uniqueness, will only seek out a facilitator who has previous experience with libraries. The truth is, they would be much more successful if they select an individual who has experience with the specific *issues* that tend to hold an organization back and keep it from making the strides it should be making. If in fact the library manager views his or her library as a corporation with a single product offering, information, he or she will understand that the corporate structure, goals, and overall mission are really no different from those of the company producing widgets. With this understanding in mind, the search for a facilitator can be much more broad, with a greater likelihood of hiring someone who can offer the tools that will provide the management team with the ability to successfully manage this small corporation called the library.

Such a retreat can serve to further the goals of the library, to focus on issues that have led to rancor or stress in the organization. The retreat can also be used to create a long-term plan or, in the case of a technology strategy (in an environment where technology changes every eighteen months), a short-term plan.

If the retreat is organized as a two-day event, staff may be invited to participate on the second day. It is important for managers to hear about the issues being dealt with by line staff. It is possible for the session to offer a comfortable level of interaction so that the staff members are able to express themselves freely. The session must not be permitted to become a whining session, but must be structured in such a manner that positive outcomes can be realized.

Finally, the retreat must not add a great deal of additional work for the participants. Encouragement must be provided to communicate and cooperate, not take advantage of colleagues. Staff must come to accept that change has become the normal state of affairs in the library, and to adapt to that change, to be curious about it, and to learn from it can be the most positive experience for any staff member.

Conferences must also be recognized for their continuing education and training opportunities. There are ample opportunities to attend and participate in local, national, and international conferences where hundreds of papers are presented, workshops and seminars are offered, and networking serves as a means by which training is accomplished. The library manager must consider sending staff to these conferences so that the habit of participating and learning becomes ingrained. Staff, of course, must understand that there are only so many dollars to support their attendance at these events, but participation in these continuing education opportunities is invaluable.

Chapter 5

Creating and Implementing a Technology Training Program for Library Staff

According to the most recent statistics provided by the American Society of Training and Development (ASTD), the top 10 percent of companies it surveyed in 2000 train 98.5 percent of employees in their organizations. The top 10 percent of companies surveyed, or "Training Investment Leaders" surveyed also spent an average of $1,547 on training per eligible employee.

Such statistics reflect library needs as much as private sector ones. As graduate schools concentrate their efforts on training MLS graduates increasingly fluent in information technology, work in the private sector becomes quite alluring. The lack of appeal for some librarians and information technologists unwilling to work in direct public service is apparent in both the public and the academic library's constant cry of short staffing.

A technology training program for library staff must be designed to address a number of these issues, not the least of which is the hiring and retention of qualified staff. Is continuing technology education and training a cure-all for the hiring and retention of library staff? Certainly not. Can it be an important element in the hiring and retention of library staff? Undoubtedly. Remember the trainer's axiom: "If you're not helping them learn, you're helping them leave." If the opportunity for staff to receive technology training on a continuous basis is accepted and promoted by the library, the rewards may well be measured in increased staff hiring and a higher retention of qualified staff, thus leading to the provision of the best customer service. Also, when familiarity and knowledge can evolve into the confidence to perform one's duties ably, life in the ever-changing environment of the library may not appear so daunting.

To be successful, the technology training program must directly respond to staff needs. Therefore, any library about to undergo the rigors of planning a fully integrated technology training program must ponder a number of questions. Some of these can be answered later through responses recorded in a technology needs assessment survey, which will be designed and administered prior to construction of the technology training program itself.

Libraries will often roll out a new program without performing adequate market research. In this instance, using the tools of market research (survey and analysis) to discover the actual technology needs of the library's internal customers will provide the program's technology training team with the most appropriate information upon which to define the training program.

Prior to this step, however, other questions must first be posed to the library administration so that their responses regarding the climate for a staff technology training program may be fully measured by the technology training team. These questions may be asked through one-on-one interviews or focus groups comprising administrators and managers. Focus groups can assist the technology training team in creating a successful survey. The questions are as follows:

1. Who is the target audience?
2. What are the staff skills?
3. What is the staff's motivation level?
4. What kind of training has staff specifically requested?
5. What kinds of definite, perceptible information is available that indicates training is needed?
6. In the past, how was training delivered?
7. Has training traditionally been on-site or off-site?
8. How successful has technology training been in the past?
9. If training has not been successful, why hasn't it?
10. Is there enough money in the budget to fund a training program?
11. Is funding incorporated into the annual budget as a regular line item, or must capital be raised to finance the program?
12. What methods of training are expected to be employed?
13. How does the staff learn most effectively?
14. What is to be included in the training program?
15. What are the successful outcomes of a training program?

Upon analysis of responses to these questions, and perhaps some direct follow-up by the technology training team as needed, a number of key activities in the planning and implementation of the program will be designed. These key activities are defined as follows:

Technology training team establishes work plan, timeline, and meeting schedule.

The team meets to establish their timeline, team duties, and meeting schedule. The team agrees to meet regularly, based on the agreed-upon timeline, in order to create, administer, analyze, and report the findings of the survey.

Examine library workplace technology.

In order to establish locations where "dedicated" classes (classes on specific topics in the library's own facilities or other training labs) would be accommodated, team site visits are necessary to discover where appropriate technology training facilities exist. A checklist of parameters is designed and used to identify facilities most appropriate and to choose sites for this aspect of the training program.

Evaluating the Technology Training Facilities

To offer the optimum technology training experience, it is clear that the *environmental* attributes of a training facility must be as accommodating and standardized as possible. When evaluating the quality of the facility, the following must be taken into account:

- Is the facility outfitted with nonglare lighting?
- Is the furniture accommodating and functional? (*Best possible scenario:* desks with cutouts for monitors angled toward students and chairs without wheels.)
- Is the temperature set at a comfortable level (not too warm, not too cold) with constant air flow?
- Is the facility soundproof?

- Are there no more than fifteen student computers in the facility?
- Is there an additional instructor workstation and an LCD projector to be used by the trainer?
- Are the sight lines to the trainer and classroom monitor clear?
- Is the equipment properly maintained and in working condition at all times?
- Are the walls of the facility bare (no posters) so that the instructor may train without distractions?
- Is there enough space on the desk for the student to place printed materials? (It is recommended to place CPUs beneath the desktop to create more workspace, if necessary.)
- Is there enough space between workstations for students to work comfortably?
- Are the monitors placed at a comfortable level on the desk?
- Are there nonglare screens on the monitors? (Protective screens are always recommended for long-term sessions at the computer.)
- Is there a "white board" in the training facility for simultaneous writing and projection on one screen? (Although an electronic white board is recommended, a large drawing board is perfectly adequate.)
- Is the facility equipped with a LAN and a dedicated T1 (or higher) data line for connection to the Internet?
- Has software been installed on the trainer's computer so that he or she can immediately access a student's computer?
- Is gentle, unobtrusive music playing prior to and during the training session designed to relax the students and allow them to concentrate? (This may be an add-on in most facilities, but studies have shown that music positively supports the learning process.)

Subsidiary Logistics

- Are there adequate parking facilities nearby or on-site? (Free or affordable?)
- Are there coffee or cold drink machines on-site or nearby?

Conduct literature searches on technology training.

Literature searches provide the team with recent articles on the design of instructional programs in the workplace. Research may reveal a wealth of statistical information on how technology training is currently being used in the workplace.

Draft a survey of technology training needs.

The survey team creates a draft of the technology needs assessment survey in the form of a questionnaire and tests it on selected staff prior to finalizing it for distribution. Sections are edited and rewritten for clarity and/or focus; then the questionnaire is reproduced in print and distributed to the entire staff. It is distributed in print because there will undoubtedly be some who would have difficulty if the survey were made available only electronically.

Conduct the survey of technology training needs.

Identification of the target audience is finalized. The technology training needs survey is delivered to all staff. The respondents are given a deadline of thirty days to return the completed questionnaires.

Compile and report findings of survey.

With an appropriately designed and targeted questionnaire, a great deal of important information can be gathered about the continuing education and training needs of the staff. The survey team analyzes not only the statistical data but the responses to the open-ended questions as well. These responses offer the survey team information that can be used not only in the design of the training program but to address other staff needs for the following fiscal year. Taking staff needs seriously and responding to them directly can also create an atmosphere of trust and an environment where the potential for promotion and retention can directly complement each other.

There are nine steps in the systematic employment of a questionnaire to be used in a survey:

1. Organize the survey team
2. Determine the survey goal

3. Select a representative sample
4. Generate the questions
5. Construct the questionnaire
6. Test the questionnaire
7. Administer the questionnaire
8. Analyze the data
9. Share and use the results

One obvious advantage to creating a questionnaire for the survey rather than conducting focus groups or direct interviews is that the questionnaire offers the respondent anonymity. This is the most appropriate means of providing the survey team with the purest responses. It is distributed and returned in such a manner that the respondents feel confident that their identities and any information they provided would remain secure.

An additional advantage of the questionnaire is that it is a very efficient means of collecting information from the point of view of the respondents. By offering distinct categorical breakdowns of information alongside a simple set of response indicators ("None, Little, Sufficient, Extensive"), it allows respondents to complete the entire questionnaire in no more than ten to fifteen minutes. Such a strategy is useful, especially when there is a large pool of potential respondents and many questions.

Other advantages of the questionnaire:

• Extremely cost effective
• Easy to analyze
• Familiarity factor for most people—less apprehension
• Reduces bias through uniformity
• Less intrusive

An example of a technology needs assessment survey appears in Appendix B.

Clarifying the nature and needs of the audience for training is one of the most important activities during the analysis phase of instructional design. The survey, then, is constructed in such a manner that respondents answer according to their perceived performance levels in terms of:

1. Skills—the ability to use one's knowledge effectively and readily in execution or performance.
2. Tasks—assigned pieces of work to be completed within a certain time.
3. Knowledge—acquaintance with or understanding of (in this case) specific hardware/software applications.

Since library staff have such disparate job titles and functions, the goal in constructing the survey is to make certain it is built for clarity and ease of use. Also, it is important to ascertain the range of abilities, from the simplest to the most esoteric. This is done so that a comprehensive technology training program may be designed that is applicable to all library staff including top management, middle management, professional librarians, paraprofessionals, clerical and support staff, facilities staff, and part-time employees.

Draft, review, and finalize technology training curriculum.

The instructional design team creates a comprehensive, fully integrated technology training program.

Identify, study, and select technology training vendors.

Vendors are contacted and interviewed with the intent of creating a fully integrated technology training program. In terms of the course offerings, it is important for the technology training team to develop a program that offers courseware both online and through live delivery that complements each other in content, look, and feel. Final selections are made and contracts signed.

Promote technology training program.

Activities to promote the program may include:

- Site visits to member libraries
- Presentations at annual and committee meetings
- Web site promotion on home page
- Training administrator meetings
- Campaign strategy meetings with vendors
- Promotional material handouts
- E-mail reminders

Implementation of the technology training program.

The challenge of creating a fully integrated technology training program is to identify the various elements that intersect with one another so that staff are fully brought into the process. Staff must be offered the opportunity to receive continuing education and training whenever required.

Technology Training: An Integrated Approach

According to the American Society for Training and Development, approximately 18.7 percent of training is presently being delivered via "learning technologies" (Web, satellite, computer-based).[1] Thus, any training program must be built with this means of service delivery included. However, since there are a number of staff who do not find self-directed training productive, there must also be an instructor-led component so that the program remains inclusive. Thus, the library's instructional design team must take into account that an integrated technology training program has the best opportunity to achieve positive results. The elements of this integrated approach include:

- *Web-based training* (online training delivered via the Web that may be accessed anywhere, anytime, available either through self-paced tutorial modules or through instructor-led tutorials).
- *Dedicated* class training (dedicated classes are specific classes on a specific topic held in a technology training facility in selected school locations).
- *Voucher* class training (voucher classes are those for which a certain number of individual vouchers are purchased so that staff may attend a class at their convenience held at a vendor's facility).

A technology vendor (or vendors) is identified, offering the ability to provide instructor-led technology training including a dedicated class training curriculum and a voucher-supported training schedule. A vendor (or vendors) with the ability to offer a complete Web-based training solution is identified. The Web-based training vendor must provide the following deliverables:

- Electronic "preassessment" evaluation so that users may gauge their strong and weak points prior to registering for any particular training module.
- Electronic "postassessment" so that the users (and administrators) may gauge the success of each student.
- The most comprehensive selection of technology training courses available.
- A plan must be in place for the vendor to offer courses that can be downloaded so that they may be taken at the user's convenience.
- Courses must be accessible for reference purposes so users need not take an entire course in order to answer a reference question.
- Courses must be able to be taken as many times as the user desires.
- Courses must be available for continuing education unit credits (CEUs).
- An electronic reference library must be available so users may consult recognized reference sources for assistance when necessary.
- There must be an electronic and live "help desk" to assist users.
- There must be a selection of instructor-led classes as well as self-study courses so users may select the manner by which they may be more effectively trained.
- The vendor must offer a selection of new courses each month so users may avail themselves of the latest in technology training opportunities.
- In order for the library manager to propose a fully integrated technology training program, the vendor supplying Web-based training must furnish courses that provide content integration with the vendor offering dedicated and voucher courses.
- A Web-based technology training program curriculum must be comprehensive and inclusive to appeal to staff with few skills as well as to staff with substantial skills.

In selecting the vendor who will provide the instructor-led training component of the program, the following elements must be considered:

- The vendor must provide classes whose courseware is synchronous with that being offered by the Web-based training vendor.

- Instructors must be certified to teach their specialties.
- Dedicated classes may not be larger than fifteen students.
- In the case of a library system whose coverage area may be vast, the vendor must offer voucher training classes that are accessible within or close to the coverage area.
- Because staff turnover is fairly constant, the vendor must offer technology training to replacement staff at a cost of *only* the courseware.
- To retain flexibility in the technology training program, staff must be able to attend training with the use of a voucher at a vendor facility anywhere in the country.
- If necessary, staff must be able to repeat a class where a voucher has been redeemed at no cost.
- As with Web-based training, the vendor must offer pre- and postassessment testing with each class attended.

Prior to the Official Rollout

A training administrator (TA) for each site must be identified to serve as the communications liaison. The TA's primary responsibility is to serve as the information and communications conduit between staff at their particular location and the lead TA. Education of the TAs begins with an informational kickoff meeting held approximately one month prior to the official program rollout. This meeting will include the lead TA, local TAs, and the vendors. The goals of this meeting are as follows:

- Explain the project plan
- Agree on goals
- Explore the vendor offerings
- Explain TA responsibilities
- Identify contacts
- Distribute e-mail and telephone contact list
- Discuss maximum use of communication tools
- Identify and find solutions for any barriers to implementation
- Finalize timeline for implementation
- Lead TA and local TAs will schedule on-site training for interested staff

Approximately two weeks prior to the rollout, the staff will be invited to attend a training session at each location where the lead TA will moderate a presentation on the integrated technology training program.

During the negotiation phase of the project, vendors must agree to work with the training team to assist in establishing a publicity campaign to support it. A strong publicity rollout at the outset of the program will yield invaluable results over the life of the program.

Besides serving as communications liaison between the lead TA and the staff, the local TA's secondary responsibility is to serve as the "champion" of the integrated technology training program. This task is continuous and is of great importance to the success of the program. The local TA shoulders the responsibility of promoting the values of the program to staff and may wish to use various promotional tools to do so, including the following:

- Regular e-mails promoting the value to staff of the program.
- Distribute flyers and post them prominently as a regular reminder of the program.
- Sponsor special events where there will be a speaker (perhaps the TA) touting the values of the program.
- Hold a drawing for the staff members completing the most courses.
- Have districts compete for highest percentage of registered employees. The winning district receives a reward.

Management of the Program

- The overall management of the program must be established at lead TA level in cooperation with the vendors selected and the technology training team.
- Reporting and evaluation of the technology training program must begin upon implementation of the program.
- The variety of reports will be explored and, based upon need and reporting requirements, numerous reports can be generated for any required time period to track usage of deliverables offered in the program.

- Statistical reporting may be generated utilizing reporting mechanisms built into the vended course product.
- Reports generated must be electronically available to all library administrations and available online through the library's Web reporting mechanism.

Conclusion

The technology training program must be designed to respond to the following measurable outcomes:

- Library staff will receive overall technology training and technology integration training to improve their ability to integrate technology into their daily workflow.
- A technology training deployment plan will provide library staff with tools and training necessary to use the Internet and software programs to satisfy the overall core competencies expected by the library organization.
- The library staff's growing experience and comfort with the Internet and software programs in the library will increase their usage of technology.

Library staff will benefit from continuous technology training that will improve their ability to interact with their internal and external customers.

Chapter 6

Evaluating a Technology Training Program for Library Staff

At the end of the first quarter of the fiscal year in which the technology training program is active, the design team begins preparations to create and administer an evaluation survey. In an effort to get information directly from staff members who took classes in the technology training program, the survey design team creates an evaluation survey and delivers it to each individual who took either a Web-based training class or any of the instructor-led courses held either at the vendor's facility or the library's own facility.

It is fair to say that the comprehensive result of evaluating the efficiency of any training program is to discover its overall effectiveness. Key outcomes of the program must be examined to ascertain whether what was learned was used to directly serve customer needs. Have library staff who participated in the program gained increased knowledge in order to achieve maximum levels of performance? Have they gained the confidence necessary to carry out direct service functions to both internal and external customers, knowing that they have received appropriate training in the technological skills expected of them by the public?

As important as these questions are to library staff participating in the training program, it is equally important for the technology training team to understand what particular areas of training might have been missed. To plan a continuing education and training program for future years, it remains important for the technology training team to understand what was most useful in the program and what was not.

To obtain raw data to be used for the evaluation of the technology training program for library staff, a survey is designed:

- *Survey instrument:* A questionnaire with multiple-choice questions and open-ended questions.

- *Administration:* The questionnaire is delivered to individuals who have taken part in the technology training program.
- *Distribution:* The distribution of the questionnaires is classified by the following personnel categories: Administrative Staff, Technical Services, Public Services, Other.

Case Study: The SEFLIN Technology Training Program for Library Staff

The Southeast Florida Library Information Network (SEFLIN) technology training program was designed as a fully integrated one combining instructor-led training at vendor facilities, dedicated classes taught by fully qualified technology trainers held at selected SEFLIN member institutions' computer training facilities, and, finally, online training, in which staff were able to take courses through a contracted Web-based training initiative.

Staff members accessed hundreds of training courses through the program. The word "access" is a key element in a fair evaluation of the means by which the program was utilized by staff. Since individuals all learn differently, it becomes paramount for the evaluation team to understand by what methods the training is being used. Instructor-led training courses are full-day ones where an individual receives specific training in a single subject in a very concentrated session. On the other hand, online training courses are accessible whenever an individual can find the opportunity to log into an individual account from any computer. Online courses were accessed not only for an individual to complete an entire learning module on a specific subject, but were also used heavily either for reference purposes or to support knowledge gained by taking instructor-led courses. Thus, entire courses were taken more often with instructors than online. Through monthly analysis of usage statistics, it became quite clear that the online training courses served as a very important reference and support tool for those seeking information about the operation of a particular software package. Also, since the online vendor also offered a virtual reference library that could be accessed by staff, these reference materials were frequently used in lieu of purchasing or borrowing the print books when necessary.

A sample list of the classes accessed by staff through the SEFLIN technology training program included the following:

Access 2000: Advanced
Access 2000: Introduction to Application Development
Access 2000: Level 1
Access 2000: Level 2
Access 7.0: Introduction
Access 97: Advanced
Access 97: Introduction to Application Development
Access 97: Level 1
Access 97: Level 2
Acrobat 4: Basic Skills
ACT! 2000: Introduction
Approach Millennium Edition 9.0: Introduction
Excel 2000: Advanced
Excel 2000: Level 1
Excel 7.0: Advanced
Excel 7.0: Introduction
Excel 97: Advanced
Excel 97: Level 1
Excel 97: Level 2
FileMaker Pro 5.0: Introduction
FreeHand 9: Level 3
FrontPage 2000: Advanced
FrontPage 2000: Introduction
FrontPage 98: Introduction
GroupWise 5.5: Advanced
GroupWise 5.5: Introduction
HTML 4.01 Web Authoring: Level 1
HTML 4.01 Web Authoring: Level 2
HTML Programming 4.0: Advanced
HTML Programming 4.0: Introduction
Internet Explorer 4.0: Introduction
Internet Explorer 5.0: Introduction
Internet Explorer 5.5: Introduction
Internet Explorer 5.5: Introduction (British English)
Introduction to Personal Computers Using Windows 98
Lotus 1-2-3 Millennium Edition 9.0: Level 1
Macintosh OS 9.0: Introduction
Microsoft Encarta 2000: Overview
Microsoft Internet Information Server 4.0
Microsoft Money 2000

Microsoft Money 2001
Microsoft Office 2000: Document Integration
Microsoft Office 2000: Macro Programming Using VBA
Microsoft Office 2000: New Features
Microsoft Office 97: Document Integration
Microsoft Office 97: Small Business Tools
Microsoft PhotoDraw 2000 Version 2.0: Introduction
Microsoft Project 2000: Level 1
Microsoft Project 98: Advanced
Microsoft Project 98: Introduction
Microsoft Publisher 2000: Introduction
Microsoft Vizact 2000: Introduction
Microsoft Works Suite 2000: Introduction
NetMeeting 3.0: Internet Conferencing
NetObjects Fusion 4.5
Netscape Communicator 4.5: Introduction
Netscape Communicator 4.7: Introduction
Notes 4.5: Introduction
Notes 5.0: Mail Features
Outlook 2000: Advanced
Outlook 2000: Introduction
Outlook 97: Introduction
Outlook 98: Advanced
Outlook 98: Introduction
Overview of Encarta Encyclopedia 2001
Paradox 9.0: Advanced
Paradox 9.0: Introduction
Picture It! Publishing 2001
PowerPoint 2000: Advanced
PowerPoint 2000: Introduction
PowerPoint 7.0: Introduction
PowerPoint 97: Introduction
QuarkXPress 4.0: Basic Skills 1
QuarkXPress 4.0: Basic Skills 2
Quattro Pro 9.0: Charts and Databases
Quattro Pro 9.0: Spreadsheets
QuickBooks 2000: Get Going
Quicken 2000: Introduction
Quicken 2001: Introduction

Quicken 99: Introduction
Relational Database Design: A Practical Approach
Streets & Trips 2001
Visio 2000 Professional: Basic Skills
Windows 2000: Introducción (Español)
Windows 2000: Introduction
Windows 2000: Network and Operating System Basics
Windows 2000: Transition from Windows 98
Windows 2000: Transition from Windows 98 (Chinese)
Windows 95: Advanced
Windows 95: Introduction
Windows 98: Introducción (Español)
Windows 98: Introduction
Windows 98: Selected Features and Internet Options
Windows 98: Transition from Windows 95
Windows Millennium Edition: Introduction
Windows NT Workstation 4.0: Introduction
Word 2000: Advanced
Word 2000: Level 1
Word 2000: Level 2
Word 2000: Niveau 1 (Dutch)
Word 2000: Nivel 1 (Spanish/English)
Word 7.0: Level 1
Word 97: Advanced
Word 97: Level 1
Word 97: Level 2
WordPerfect 8.0: Level 1
WordPerfect 8.0: Level 2
WordPerfect 9.0: Level 1
WordPerfect 9.0: Level 2

The breadth of courses taken in whole or part satisfied the technology training team in terms of having provided the library staff with the largest possible selection of course offerings. In its first year, the program sought to demonstrate the value of a fully integrated and well-orchestrated technology training program. To this end, with the intentions of the technology training team in mind, the evaluation survey sought the following outcomes:

- To measure the users' assessment of the SEFLIN Technology Training Program
- To ascertain key demographics of users
- To appraise skill levels before and after training (knowledge and confidence)
- To seek out support for and barriers to learning
- To discover direct learning impact measures
- To measure the program's delivery methods
- To measure the program's content impact
- To seek suggestions for changes and improvement of program

The survey questionnaire (see Appendix B) was designed and then distributed to staff. The survey responses that were received represented a cross-section of staff that had participated in parts of the program, dedicated courses, voucher/vendor courses or online classes, or in all segments of the program. Responses provided the technology training team with ample raw data from which to comment.

Key highlights of the survey responses to the multiple choice questions were as follows:

- 52 percent of the respondents were holders of the MLS degree
- 70 percent of the responses were from public libraries
- 47 percent of the respondents had more than ten years of service
- 26 percent of the respondents had more than twenty years of service
- Knowledge/skill levels *before* taking training: 67 percent
- Knowledge/skill levels *after* taking training: 92 percent
- Confidence/ability to use technical skills learned in training program: 65 percent
- Had the time to use technical skills learned in training program: 70 percent
- Able to access library resources to apply knowledge learned: 83 percent
- Training program improved *daily* performance on the job: 87 percent
- Training program improved *overall* job performance: 84 percent
- Effectiveness of delivery methods: voucher classes, 93 percent; dedicated classes, 86 percent; online learning, 81 percent
- Overall program design and delivery: excellent, 55 percent; good, 38 percent; average, 5 percent

Highlights of survey responses to open-ended questions were as follows:

- What is the single most important recommendation or general recommendation(s) for improving the quality of the program? (top three responses received)
  1. Better library support for training (19 percent)
  2. More time for training (14 percent)
  3. More advanced sessions (14 percent)
- How have users been better served by your attending the technology training program? (top three responses)
  1. Learned skills to help work better with users (32 percent)
  2. Gained greater confidence to work with users (27 percent)
  3. Training taught additional/useful skills to assist in working with users (19 percent)
- Other Comments? (top three responses)
  1. Excellent service overall (18 percent)
  2. Voucher program excellent (14 percent)
  3. Online courses greatly assist learning (14 percent)

Evaluating the Overall Responses

Measuring the survey responses against the intended outcomes created a number of interesting conclusions. For example, in the area of key demographics, a portrait of the respondent clearly emerged. By virtue of the responses received, a profile of the average library staff participant in the SEFLIN technology training program may be drawn as follows:

- Employed in a public library
- Held an MLS
- Worked in public services (reference, circulation, etc.)
- Accessed all types of training equally (voucher, dedicated, online)
- Worked in libraries more than twenty years

It was a bit disturbing to note that while staff holding an MLS were in the majority of those who responded to the evaluation survey, monthly statistics gathered by the technology training team suggested that the overwhelming majority of staff enrolled in training did not hold an MLS.

Perhaps the most pleasant surprise to the technology training team was the magnitude of the positive impact on library staff that had worked in SEFLIN member libraries for a number of years. If there ever was a notion that only younger staffers are willing to keep up with technology and that long-time staffers are not willing to change with the times, one only has to consider the responses in this category, where 47 percent of respondents overall who participated in the technology training program had worked in libraries longer than eleven years.

Equally gratifying were the levels of knowledge and confidence gained by staff through the program. For example, the overall knowledge and skill levels increased 25 percent after in the program. The confidence levels in terms of improved daily and overall performance measures were well into the 80 percent range, certainly statistics that clearly support a direct learning impact on staff.

It was also important to seek suggestions on how to tailor the program even closer to staff needs. Allowing survey respondents to suggest ways to improve the process empowers individuals to become an integral part of that process. Therefore the open-ended questions solicited responses that can be acted upon not only by the technology training team of SEFLIN but by the individual libraries as well. For example, when staff suggest that they would like to have "better library support for training," that implies that they would like to have more time and technological and philosophical support for training. This also supports the sentiment that libraries should include an increased training line in their annual budgets to further support the training needs of their staff.

According to this survey, library staff are eager and willing to increase their knowledge and skills. Perhaps one of the most satisfying statistics that emerged from this survey, in terms of program delivery methods, was the high number of library staff who registered for online technology training. In the SEFLIN evaluation survey, 48 percent of respondents stated that they were accessing their training online. Given the fact that online training is a relatively new wrinkle in the library training universe, this statistic certainly appears to support the concept that library staff are not willing to operate behind the technological curve. They are more than willing and able to stand squarely in front of it, providing the customers with the most knowledgeable and skillful information service available.

The complete statistical results of the SEFLIN Technology Training Outcomes Survey may be viewed by visiting <http://www.seflin.org/academy/results-of-eval.html>.

Chapter 7

Clicks and Bricks

In 1999 and early 2000, a cliché, or rather a mantra, was being chanted by stock market gurus over and over again, ad nauseam. It went something like, "the U.S. economy is engaged in a struggle between the old economy and the new." Businesses that constitute the "old" economy are the so-called basic materials that made the twentieth century the "American century": paper, steel, utilities, aluminum, general manufacturing and heavy industry, industries that powered America through the world wars and into its fantastically prosperous peace.

For decades, the rallying cries of investors included "What's good for U.S. Steel is good for America" or "You'll never go wrong with Coca-Cola." Investors put their faith in those statements and their money into those stocks and were rewarded over the long term with a steady stream of profits and dividend checks every quarter for decades. Slow and steady investing was the counsel from our fathers. But then came the "new" economy.

The Internet arrived, and with it an entirely new group of stocks in which to invest. Investment houses supported these untried companies and promoted the stocks using the philosophy that the economy was shifting into a new paradigm, one that suggested that we would never slide back into the old manner of doing business again. All shopping would be done online. Everything would be available on the Internet, especially information housed in libraries, and we would never look back. We would only move forward. With progress would come the death of the old economic models. The "long-term" outlook for investors in new-economy stocks was shortened from years to a few weeks. Investment sectors such as semiconductors, wireless telecom, computer hardware, software, portals, and Internet stocks of all kinds helped to create and just as quickly demolish the largest class of millionaires in the country's history. In slightly more than a year, America witnessed the emergence, the highs, the lows, and the crash of so many dot coms that the ride was nauseating. The Internet and the new economic bubble had burst. The technological revolution had certainly brought about a world of change. But rather than becoming the panacea for all that was wrong with the old economy, to the world of business, the new technologies had simply become another means by which to engage in commerce.

Approximately half of all American families now hold some investment in the stock market. Just prior to the bursting of the Internet bubble, many investors were swayed by the hype that supported this radical change in the economy. Many thought of it simply as a means of getting rich quickly. The questionable nature of these new-economy stocks, with their equally questionable business models, was seen every day in the stock market's wild swings up and down. A number of economists suggested that the old economic model whereby companies and their stocks are valued must be discarded in favor of a model that measures the *potential* of future profits. The more conservative brokers and investors considered this investment strategy not really investing, but outright gambling. Others suggested that the only way the new-economy companies and their stocks could be evaluated was by their future growth potential, not their present ability (or lack of ability) to generate real profits. Investing on the *expectation* of profits turned out to be as ridiculous a premise as it sounded. Still, the price of new-economy stocks soared and the party continued.

The old-economy pundits maintained all along that unless there was a real profit on the company's balance sheet, the company simply could not survive. The new-economy oracles, however, suggested that the old models must be thrown out and new ones established in order to value a company and its stock properly. They decreed that buildings (bricks and mortar) would disappear in favor of *virtual* structures, where one could simply click a mouse and obtain nearly every product and service available. That too, turned out to be a false premise, and a completely mistaken one.

Early on in the euphoria of the Internet revolution, it was proposed by Internet venture capitalists that "businesses are currently replacing inventories with information" or "they are moving from bricks to clicks." What did those statements actually mean? It meant that retail establishments are replacing their stores (the bricks) with online stores (the clicks) that offer *information* on their inventories, first rather than their actual inventories. In a manner of speaking, this is analogous to the painting by René Magritte titled *La Trahison des Images* (1929), which includes the words *"Ceçi n'est pas une pipe"* (This is not a pipe). The work is a painting of a smoker's pipe. In reality it is *not* a pipe. It is a *painting* of a pipe. When a retail store, then, offers products online, they are not really offering products per se, but information on those products.

When you order that item, it arrives, and you hold it in your hand, then you are in possession of the actual item, and not until then. The rest has simply been word play. The experts suggested that instead of going to a store to purchase a widget, you would have to go to a Web site and find out about that widget. But what if you are not that knowledgeable and you are, in a manner of speaking, comparison shopping for an item? To examine that item from all sides, by eye, not even a 360 degree camera view of that item on your screen will be sufficient. You see only the illusion of that item, not its reality. Then, after you receive the item and finally examine it, it may not even be acceptable to you. So, essentially, when Internet companies boast about their products being available through their Web site, information about those products is essentially all they are offering. If a product arrives at your door and you are unhappy with it, you must make certain that you have carefully read the company's returns policy in order to accomplish a successful return, reorder, and, perhaps, refund of that item. So, the returns policy becomes another piece of information with which the consumer must become familiar.

In the case of certain businesses whose products are already in the form of information, such as books, periodicals, CDs, videos, DVDs, and the like, it is perfectly acceptable to sample an item before you purchase it. You can read excerpts from a book or listen to a bit of a CD before buying. If you are a knowledgeable consumer and have already gone to the store to look at a certain item and previously held it in your hands and used it, you will then be familiar enough with that item to confidently obtain it online. But what is the point? You could have purchased that item when you were in the store in the first place. This is where the Internet marketplace began to crumble. The incorporation of Web-based services through many of the major retail outlets has been slow and stumbling. Many a "clicks" operation has been forced to resort to "old" economic models to accomplish successful product delivery. Shoppers like to shop. They like to handle an item.

They like to see it is real before they buy. They do not just want information about that item. So, the dot com economy began to slip away as shoppers abandoned the clicks in favor of the bricks.

Now that the smoke has cleared, it is obvious that, rather than replacing bricks, the clicks will be incorporated into every business model to facilitate business. The library manager, too, must recognize that there must be a balance between the two in order to offer the customer the most comprehensive library service available. Libraries today have their own versions of old economy versus new. If customers expect all of a library's services to be available electronically, for the time being at least, they harbor unrealistic expectations. While library managers must reorganize the annual budget to include more electronic products and less print, print products are still demanded by the library customer.

Even the library building itself is expected to continue to serve as an anchor in the community. More than 85 percent of library bond issues were passed in communities across the country in 1999. That percentage clearly proves a community's need for the library as a physical entity, even for those who do not borrow books.

The library building itself continues to represent a place where one can go not only for information, but for leisure programs, seminars, business meetings, book discussions, arts and crafts, children's story time, and all of the activities traditionally offered by the library. The community demands that the library provide a center to the community, a vital link to the people living in the community.

There remains in the library, as in the commercial world, a need for people to network with other people. While information delivery systems move more toward an electronic delivery environment, the community will battle to retain its library buildings because of all of the basic personal and people services they provide. The library manager seeking to modernize his or her institution will be wise to recognize the indispensability of balance. Today, maintaining that balance is a tricky and sometimes difficult maneuver. But to serve the customer in such a time of change, the ability to achieve that balance is one of the most important qualities a library manager can bring to the job. A report titled *Buildings, Books and Bytes,* released by the Washington-based Benton Foundation, focuses upon the importance of the library as a physical entity in every community. This report is an invaluable tool for the library manager's understanding of the importance of the library within the community and in what manner the shift toward digital delivery of information will impact the library and the community it serves.[1]

The library may deliver its product either through its bricks outlet, its building, or through its clicks outlet, electronic access, and either will be acceptable, because the library's product (i.e., information) may be obtained by either format. Libraries can more easily combine the old and the new economies in their business models, ostensibly with less difficulty than their commercial counterparts, because of the nature of the product they deliver. However, libraries are faced with the same quandary over the percentage of clicks and bricks required to most effectively deliver their product.

As the circulation of materials in libraries continues to decrease, or at best remain flat, attendance and usage of in-house services, especially computers, continues to increase. The library must keep its budgets fluid in order to accommodate the manner in which the public accesses its product.

But what must the library manager take into consideration for such an accomodation? Where, for example, does a new building or a building renovation fit in this scheme? Is it wise to build a new library in the face of massive economic upheaval and change in the way services are delivered? According to *Library Journal*'s annual architectural survey, there is still generous support for both the old and the new economies in terms of both bricks and clicks.[2] For example, support for library renovations, new construction, and bond issues for new construction remains strong. It is clear that the library, while still in the center of the public's consciousness in its value to the community, must provide, inside that new building, services that enhance electronic access as much as larger program and multimedia material space.

Today, the taxpayer and legislator rarely fail to support a measure to build a new library. However, in an era of high expectations, libraries must offer faster, better, and more current information services and the knowledgeable staff to accommodate those needs or, unlike the past, those who can afford it will go elsewhere to fulfill their needs. If, for example, a customer is equipped with a high-speed computer and fiber optic phone line at home, he or she can easily access hundreds of free information databases to fill any information need. Likewise, using a strong search engine, that customer can access more than a trillion pages of information on millions of subjects, from practical to intellectual, without the use of the library's resources. He or she may also purchase books online from a variety of commercial sources.

For the well-heeled customer, the library is simply the site of last resort for hard-to-find items, current fiction, and a building necessary to support the stability of the community. To serve this customer, the library must offer remote access not only to its online public access catalog (OPAC) but to other OPACs as well (university, other public libraries, etc.) along with a host of specialized, freely accessible subscription databases as well as a strong print collection. Still, the library may have already lost this level of customer. Conversely, the customer (whether public library customer or academic student of little means) who does not own a home computer and requires books that are too expensive to purchase must continue to use a strong library collection (both print and electronic) as well as additional services that can be found inside the library building itself. While clicks are clearly gaining ground, bricks are as necessary to the library experience as they ever were.

Chapter 8

The Challenge of the Virtual Library

The escalation in the library customer's demand for access to electronic resources has library administrators considering and implementing the creation of the all-electronic, full-service "virtual library." As the information needs of the general public have become ever more sophisticated, the ability to obtain easy access not only to reference resources, but to *all* library services electronically has become a major expectation of the library customer. Therefore, whether it is virtual or traditional, any service that can be offered from the library, excluding perhaps actually taking possession of a borrowed book, must be available to all.

Wendy Pradt Lougee of the University of Michigan has written,

> Technology has evolved to a point where it has had a tremendously democratizing effect in its distributed form, with the potential to alter dramatically the roles of the various stakeholders in communication, publishing, and the generation of information. Indeed, theoretically anyone can serve as "publisher" in the dissemination of knowledge. Anyone can amass and organize resources and declare himself or herself a "library." These forces have also stressed and altered the traditional linear processes that move works from author to publisher to library, and they could alter the library's relative position in these linear processes.[1]

The concept of the virtual library has been deliberated and, in a mounting number of institutions, successfully developed over the course of the past decade. Today, there are "virtual libraries," "digital libraries," "libraries without walls," or the like, on every subject from gardening to fish. Although most of these libraries have been developed by academic and corporate entities, public libraries and library consortia are examining their viability as well. Today, however, so many libraries are either constructing these virtual libraries or at least considering building one that a respectable library of literature has already been published on the subject (see the bibliography).

Despite the fact that these terms have often been used interchangeably, there is a clear distinction between the concept of the "virtual" and the "digital" library. The digital library has been described as an entity that basically stores materials in electronic format and manipulates large collections of those materials effectively.

The virtual library, on the other hand, has been defined as:

- " . . . an organized set of links to items on the network"[2]
- "Directories with resources that librarians or cybrarians have organized in a logical way."[3]

The Santa Fe Workshop on Distributed Knowledge Work Environments has more accurately defined the concept of the virtual library as "not merely equivalent to a digitized collection with information management tools. It is rather an environment to bring together collections, services, and people in support of the full life cycle of creation, dissemination, use, and preservation of data, information and knowledge."[4]

In the most comprehensive and practical model, a virtual library can combine the best electronic resources with traditional library services such as ready reference, document delivery, renewals, library card registration, reciprocal borrowing, and instant access to community information using as few mouse clicks as possible. "The library's broad responsibility [is] to make sense of the environment of information to its users—no longer focused simply on description and categorization, but increasingly challenged to bring order, coherence, usability, and integration to our physical and virtual libraries."[5]

The virtual library was originally developed to serve the academic community. As it became necessary for university researchers to access an increasing number of electronic resources, the concept was initiated to fill that need. Users could log onto a single organized site and click from resource to resource, solving their individual research queries.

The library administrator must consider the virtual library as an *extension* of existing services rather than an addition to them. The virtual library must not serve as a replacement for libraries seeking a solution to problematic traditional library functions.

As the virtual library becomes reality, an administrative development team must regularly survey electronic resources for possible addition to the available resources. Review sites for electronic resources are increasing, and evaluation of these resources serves as the team's primary reference source for appropriate content. A selection of these sites follows:

<http://www.vuw.ac.nz/~agsmith/evaln/evaln.htm>
<http://lii.org>
<http://scout.cs.wisc.edu/report/sr/current/>
<http://www.sitesource.com>
<http://www.ifla.org/II/etext/htm>
<http://www.unc.edu/cit/infobits/index.html>
<http://www.clearinghouse.net>
<http://sunsite.berkeley.edu/KidsClick!/>

The following selected list of active virtual libraries includes several sites that already offer an excellent fusion of fulfillment of customer need combined with the best professional resource selection:

- *The Internet Public Library,* <http://www.ipl.org/>—considered the best virtual library of its kind presently operating. By clicking on their "Collections" link, one is transported to a search directory supported by thousands of excellent sources.
- *Project Bartleby,* <http://www.bartleby.com/>—a privately held company that offers access to tens of thousands of books in full-text over the Web.
- *Project Gutenberg,* <http://promo.net/pg/>—the virtual library of literary content, with more than 10,000 works online.
- *American Memory,* <http://memory.loc.gov/ammem/amhome.html>—the Library of Congress's massive undertaking of digitizing and making available virtual library of their multimedia collections.
- *California Digital Library,* <http://www.cdlib.org/>—Access to more than 14 million items across nine campuses of University of California.

Along with the growing number of virtual libraries, a number of serious issues arise. Since the concept is barely a decade old, it appears to be premature to sound the death knell for the planet's brick and mortar libraries, especially since *more* libraries are being built today, not fewer. However, one view, perhaps several years into the future, suggests we at least consider these issues:

- If electronic access is accepted as a viable replacement for print by funding agencies, will print libraries disappear in favor of virtual libraries?
- Will publishers eventually produce everything they publish electronically *instead* of in print? Can they afford to produce both as costs increase?
- Will the copyright laws continue to be rewritten and refined in order to accommodate violations in electronic access? Is the Digital Millennium Copyright Act enough?
- Will the number of electronic database publishers decline as more material can be accessed freely through other means?
- Is fair use an acceptable fallback position for virtual libraries to justify linking to copyrighted sites for free?
- What will it mean for the royalties of individual copyright holders who have written material that is being linked around the world through virtual libraries?
- Can public libraries adequately justify funding such an endeavor? Can they afford not to?

The Consortial Perspective

A multitype library consortium (MLC) will approach the creation of a virtual library from a unique perspective. As the membership of the MLC may include public, academic, school, and special libraries with vastly different needs, building a virtual entity that can adequately serve all of its members is a challenge. "The consortial virtual library is more of a superset of the traditional library than a subset. [It] deals with collections and services, and includes both digital and non-digital resources. The consortial virtual library as a complex organization that offers a range of services."[6]

A virtual library created by an MLC has no tangible counterpart within the consortium. Its primary value is to offer the user a single service point from which to perform a broadcast search of the OPACs of member libraries as well as all licensed or free databases selected for the virtual library. The most familiar means by which to present a broadcast search is through the Z39.50 information retrieval protocol. The National Information Standards Institute (NISO), an accredited standards developer that serves the library, information, and publishing communities, approved the original standard in 1988. Basically, it defines a standard way for two computers to communicate for the purpose of information retrieval. Z39.50 makes it easier to use large information databases by standardizing the procedures and features for searching and retrieving information. Specifically, Z39.50 supports information retrieval in a distributed client and server environment where a computer operating as a client submits a search request (query) to another computer acting as an information server. Software on the server performs a search on one or more databases and creates a set of records that meet the criteria of the search request as a result. The server returns records from the resulting set to the client for processing. The power of Z39.50 is that it separates the user interface on the client side from the information servers, search engines, and databases. Z39.50 provides a consistent view of information from a wide variety of sources and offers client implementers the capability to integrate information from a range of databases and servers.

Another protocol developed to conduct a broadcast search is through what has been described as "prism" technology. This technology "uses a library's circulation system from any vendor as a springboard to the databases for simultaneous searches of all the facility's resources . . . it enables you to search any or all when resources that are hotlinked on the library's web site at the same time with one interface."[7]

Since it is unlikely that the libraries that are members of the MLC have all engaged the same integrated library system (ILS) vendor, there must be appropriate technologies to search each ILS and return as uniform a result as possible. There must also be a vibrant and exciting design so that the look and feel of the front end of the virtual library is appealing as well as functional.

A virtual library of this sort creates a value-added service for members and potential users of an MLC in the form of a "union catalog" that will include all of the OPACs of the member libraries. With the addition of selected appropriate databases that may be searched through a single interface, the virtual library of the MLC may offer a service that has no tangible counterpart.

Conclusion

Questions of clarity, content, and copyright must be considered by the library administrator should he or she embark on the construction of a virtual library. While a number of library professionals have been comfortable with the concept of the virtual library as simply another means of defining their own digital collections as opposed to their print collections, it is clear that the full-blown version is much more. Today, as an increasing amount of content is conceived directly in digital format, the design of the virtual library is as important as the design of the physical one. Building the virtual library is little different than building the brick and mortar variety. The planning that goes into supporting the construction of the former must be equal to the labor of giving birth to the latter.

Chapter 9

The Library Consortium

While large libraries and systems benefit from their size and their ability to provide many services, a small library can find a great deal of strength and support as a member of a library consortium. Library consortia offer the small and medium-size library a number of beneficial centralized services such as:

- Centralized interlibrary loan
- Staff continuing education and training
- Special materials cataloging
- Daily courier services
- Information technology consulting
- Information maintenance assistance
- A consortium-maintained OPAC
- Consortium-negotiated licensed databases
- Timely reporting on all services
- Consortium annual report
- Closer connection to other member libraries in the consortium

Library consortia have also been organized not only for public libraries, but for academic libraries as well. The multitype library consortium, a hybrid organization of public, academic, and even private libraries, serves a wide range of issues as a single entity.

Although the library pays an annual fee to the consortium for these centralized services, many headaches can be eliminated for the library manager. For example, the time needed to negotiate a vendor contract with each and every online database provider and/or automated circulation system vendor might be enough to convince the library manager to investigate the value of joining a consortium. Also, staff training can be offered through the consortium at a discount and perhaps at a central location if the consortium maintains a training facility at its headquarters. The library manager should develop a plan for consortium membership and a cost analysis pointing out the potential value of joining.

In recent years there has been a rise in the number of competing consortia, which will undoubtedly lead to consolidation. Arnold Hirshon, the executive director of the Northeast Library Information Network (NELINET) has noted "that censorial consolidation will intensify in the near future, in part because an individual library will not be able to continue investing time, expertise, and money into more than two or three consortia."[1]

On the other side of this issue, there are library managers who feel strongly that by joining a consortium, they lose a certain amount of autonomy. In certain instances, that is probably true. However, all consortia have a mechanism in place in the form of a board or advisory council whose task it is to create policy for the consortium. The advisory council should include representation from a variety of the member libraries, whose vote has equal weight. The individual library need not lose its independence if it can be voted to the council or advisory board. When policies are established for the consortium, they are to be the result of the decision-making process, which includes input from each of the members so there is more opportunity to provide the best overall service to the member libraries and, therefore, to the customer.

So many library consortia have been established around the country that vendors have had to negotiate with them in regard to contract prices as never before. "Group rates" have given library consortia a power that they never could have wielded in the past. They forced the vendor's hand in offering lower rates and more enhanced packages of services, thus allowing the consortium the same bargaining power as that held by the larger multibranch systems. Such negotiations between consortium representatives and vendors have also led the vendors to develop better and more usable products to more ably serve consortia and multibranch systems. These kinds of wholesale negotiations have been extremely fruitful, especially with electronic database vendors and automated circulation system vendors.

With more and more computers being constantly added and upgraded within the library, it also becomes highly important to develop a partnership with a particular hardware vendor. Mass purchasing of computer workstations, printers, routers, and all other peripherals becomes a huge purchasing task for even a small consortium. Thus, the purchasing power of the consortium and the need to constantly upgrade equipment places the consortium in a position where they can guarantee the purchase of a certain number of units. Given the fact that computer systems are constantly becoming outmoded, it becomes a priority to have an equipment vendor that is aware of the needs of the consortium and can offer the best price and quality customer service in return for large, continuing orders.

The value of the consortium in sending representatives to the ALA national and midwinter conferences cannot be overestimated either. At the conference they can meet one-on-one with vendors (national and sometimes local reps both attend) and discuss their members' needs, wants, and expectations. They can also meet with other users of particular products (this can also be accomplished through user group meetings during the year) to assess the worth of the product.

The consortium management can also provide invaluable assistance to a new member in finding the optimum use for programs and services developed in-house. If, for example, training sessions are to be held at a member library and a curriculum must be developed, more than likely the consortium can send along a trainer who will be equipped to teach a train-the-trainer course which has been already developed to in-house staff. The consortium member library should take as much advantage of the services offered by the consortium leader as possible. The library is, after all, paying an annual fee, and based upon what is being offered, perhaps a rather hefty annual fee. Therefore, if an individual library is dealing with particular issues, the consortium leader can always be relied upon for leadership. This, of course, is not unlike the relationship between a central library and its branches, except that in this situation, the public library is not accountable to all of the policies of the consortium leader. So even if library managers believe that they are really losing some semblance of independence by joining, they really have the best of both worlds in that they can utilize the leader for whatever is necessary to best run their system *and* retain a sense of independence.

For the library manager's consultation purposes, a selected list (not at all exhaustive) of active library consortia follows:

Adventist Libraries Information Cooperative (ALICE)
 < http://www.asdal.org/alice.html>
Alliance for Innovation in Science and Technology Information
 <http://lib-www.lanl.gov/alliance/lsanm.htm>

AMIGOS Bibliographic Council, Inc.
    <http://www.amigos.org>
Appalachian Library Information Cooperative (ALICE)
    <http://library.cn.edu:8686/ALICE>
Arizona Health Information Network (AZHIN)
    <http://www.azhin.org>
Arizona University Libraries Consortium (AULC)
    <http://www.library.yale.edu/consortia/AULC.html>
ARKLink Consortium of Arkansas Academic Libraries
    <http://www.arklink-libraries.org>
Associated Colleges of the South
    <http://www.colleges.org/>
Association of Southeastern Research Libraries (ASERL)
    <http://www.aserl.org>
Bergen County Consortium for Library Service
    <http://bccls.org>
Big 12 Plus Library Consortium
    <http://www.big12plus.org>
Boston Library Consortium (BLC)
    <http://www.blc.org>
California Digital Library (CDL)
    <http://www.cdlib.org>
California State University Software and Electronic Info. Resources
(CSU-SEIR)
    <http://www.co.calstate.edu/irt/seir>
Chesapeake Information and Research Library Alliance (CIRLA)
    <http://www.cirla.org>
Chicago Library System (CLS)
    <http://www.chilibsys.org>
College Center for Library Automation (CCLA)
    <http://ccla.lib.fl.us>
Colorado Alliance of Research Libraries (CARL)
    <http://www.coalliance.org>
Combined Higher Education Software Team (CHEST)
    <http://www.chest.ac.uk/>
Committee on Institutional Cooperation (CIC) Center for Library
Initiatives
    <http://www.cic.uiuc.edu/>
A Consortium of Missouri Libraries (MOBIUS)
    <http://merlin.missouri.edu/mobius/>

Cooperative Computer Services (CCS)
  <http://www.ccs.nsls. lib.il.us>
The Council of Connecticut Academic Library Directors (CCALD)
  <http://invictus.quinnipiac.edu/ccald.html>
Council of Federal Libraries Consortium
  <http://www.nlc-bnc.ca/cfl-cbgf/consort/>
Council of Prairie and Pacific University Libraries (COPPUL)
  <http://library.usask.ca/~winter/coppul/>
Federal Library Information Network (FEDLINK)
  , <http://lcweb.loc.gov/flicc>
Fenway Library Consortium (FLC)
  <http://www.simmons.edu/flc>
Florida Center for Library Automation (FCLA)
  <http://www.fcla.edu>
Georgia Library Learning Online (GALILEO)
  <http://www.galileo.peachnet.edu>
Georgia Online Database (BOLD)
  <www.public.lib.ga.us>
ILLINET
  <http://www.library.sos.state.il.us>
Illinois Cooperative Collection Management Program (CCMP)
  <http://libws66.lib.niu.edu/ccm/index.html>
Illinois Digital Academic Llibrary (IDAL)
  <http://www.ilcso.uiuc.edu/Web/Services/IDAL/IDAL.html>
Illinois Libraries Computer Systems Organization (ILCSO)
  <http://ilcso.aiss.uiuc.edu>
Indiana Cooperative Library Services Authority (INCOLSA)
  <http://www.incolsa.net>
Kentucky Virtual Library
  <http://www.kyvl.org>
Keystone Library Network (KLN)
  <http://www.sshechan.edu/it/kln/sskln.htm>
Library of California (LOC)
  <http://www.library.ca.gov/loc>
Long Island Library Resources Council (LILRC)
  <http://www.lilrc.org>
The Louisiana Library Network (LOUIS)
  <http://louis.lsu.edu>
Massachusetts Board of Library Commissioners (MBLC)
  <http://www.mlin.lib.ma.us/>

Michigan Library Consortium
    <http://mlc.lib.mi.us>
Minitex Library Information Network
    <http://www.minitex.umn.edu>
Minnesota Library Information Network
    <http://www.heso.state.mn.us/www/mnlink/mnlink.htm>
Missouri Library Network Corporation (MLNC)
    <http://www.mlnc.org>
Missouri Research and Education Network (MORENet)
Missouri Research Consortium of Libraries (MIRACL)
Nashville Area Library Alliance (NALA)
    <http://webz.library.vanderbilt.edu:8004/>
NELINET, Inc.
    <http://www.nelinet.net>
NEOS
    <http://www.augustana.ab.ca/neos>
Network of Alabama Academic Libraries (NAAL)
    <http://webserver.dsmd.state.al.us/ache/naal.htm>
Nevada Council of Academic Libraries (NCAL)
    <http://www.library.yale.edu/consortia/NCAL.html>
New England Land Grant University Libraries
    <http://www.necop.org>
New England Law Library Consortium (NELLCO)
    <http://www.nellco.org/>
New York Comprehensive Research Libraries (NYCRL)
    <http://www.nysl.nysed.gov/nycrl>
New York Consortium of Consortia (NYCofC)
    <http://www.rpi.edu/dept/library/html/consortia/nyscoc>
New York 3Rs Directors Organization (NYTRO)
North Carolina Libraries and Virtual Education (NCLive)
    <http://www.nclive.org>
Northeast Florida Library Information Network (NEFLIN)
    <http://www.neflin.org/>
Northeast Research Libraries Consortium (NERL)
    <http://www.library.yale.edu/NERLpublic/>
Novanet, Inc.
    <http://novanet.ns.ca/>
Nylink
    <http://nylink.suny.edu/>

NYS Office of General Services, Services and Technology Group (OGS S & T)
 <http://www.ogs.state.ny.us>
Ohio Library and Information Network (OhioLINK)
 <http://www.ohiolink.edu/>
Ohio Public Library Information Network (OPLIN)
 <http://www.oplin.lib.oh.us>
Orbis
 <http://libweb.uoregon.edu/orbis/>
PALINET and Union Library Catalogue of Pennsylvania (PALINET)
 <http://www.palinet.org>
Pennsylvania Academic Library Consortium, Inc. (PALCI)
 <http://www.lehigh.edu/~inpalci>
Portland Area Library System (PORTALS)
 <http://www.portals.org>
Solinet
 <http://www.solinet.net>
Southeast Florida Library Information Network (SEFLIN)
 <http://www.seflin.org>
Southeastern Wisconsin Information Technology Exchange (SWITCH)
 <http://caspian.switchinc.org>
Southern California Electronic Library Consortium (SCELC)
 <http://calvin.usc.edu/Info/scelc/scelc.html>
Southwestern Ohio Council for Higher Education (SOCHE)
 <http://www.soche.org>
SUNYConnect
 <http://www.sunyconnect.suny.edu/)
Tampa Bay Library Consortium
 <http://www.tblc.org>
TENN-SHARE
 <http://toltec.lib.utk.edu/~tennshare>
TexShare
 <http://www.texshare.edu>
Triangle Research Libraries Network (TRLN)
 <http://www-trln.lib.unc.edu/>
TriUniversity Group of Libraries (TUG)
 <http://www.tug-libraries.on.ca/>
UNILINC Limited
 <http://www.unilinc.edu.au>

University of Texas System Knowledge Management Center (UTS KMC)
  <http://www.lib.utsystem.edu>
Utah Academic Library Consortium
  <http://www.ualc.net>
Virtual Academic Library of New Jersey (VALE)
  <http://www.valenj.org>
Virtual Library of Virginia (VIVA)
  <http://www.viva.lib.va.us>
Washington Research Library Consortium (WRLC)
  <http://www.wrlc.org>
Washington State Libraries Statewide Database Licensing Project
  <http://www.statelib.wa.gov/sdl>
Wisconsin Interlibrary Services (WILS)
  <http://www.wils.wisc.edu>

Chapter 10

Practical Library Development

It has been suggested that in the nonprofit world of the library, there is no visible bottom line. That is, there is no one number, no percentage of revenue increase the director and his team must meet, no projected profit margin that must be exceeded from the previous year that impacts upon the success or failure of the operation. Also, it has been argued that because there is no bottom line, the currency with which the library staff works is much different. Because it appears not to be a *cash* bottom line, the employee must work in an environment emphasizing favor, rather than corporate profits, to achieve success or receive the gift of promotion. Who one is close to, who one can grant favors or from whom they can be withheld often dictates whether library employees are appreciated in their own environment. Whether an employee has success in suggesting programs that increase the funding stream of the library has little impact on whether the organization survives, so suggestions that would actually make money for the library are often dismissed out of hand. Well, that was the past.

Those of us who toil daily in libraries realize that such a sentiment is about as far from the truth as could be. There is, of course, a visible bottom line. The library manager who prepares the budget is keenly aware of this, as is the municipal department who oversees the library budget and the governing agency (education department, mayor's office, Department of State, etc.) that retains the task of financial oversight.

During an era before the term "development" made its way into the everyday parlance of the nonprofit arena, outside plans to enhance the library's revenues were unheard of. Then such a pursuit was simply considered fund-raising and little or none of it was done in the public library. The term "fund-raising," a catch phrase at best, has been forced to evolve to a higher level. For as any development person understands these days, the art of fund-raising has much more to do with prospecting for and developing potential long-term donors than with achieving a goal through a single fund-raising effort. Whatever "extras" a library wished for might have only come from elective opportunities such as the generosity of a library friends group, a wealthy local donor or small business, book sales, bake sales, other special programs, and the like.

Throughout most of the twentieth century, a library's major operational funding emanated either from the local municipality through tax assessments or from the state library (or state education department) through Library Services and Construction Act (LSCA) then Library Services and Technology Act (LSTA) grants. If a capital project was necessary, the library went directly to the voters and lobbied for a bond issue to be placed on the next ballot so that special funds could be raised to accomplish the mission of that capital project. To go outside the box, so to speak, to develop a foundation in a public library or to approach corporate funding agencies is a rather recent phenomenon.

Today, however, libraries are also increasingly under pressure from their funding agencies to appeal to the private sector, not only for special purpose funds but for operational funding as well. The reality is that it is much more appealing to potential donors to provide money for a new or special project than for operational funds. Donors would much rather have their identity attached to a special project or service that they can name in their own annual reports to further their reputation rather than provide funding for basic library operations. Also, the library usually does not appear on the corporate donor's top ten list of worthy charities to provide with funding. Such restrictive giving tends to limit the kinds of corporate funding a library can apply for. Still, the funds are out there, and the creative library manager must develop prospecting techniques using existing tools to bring in those needed dollars.

More than $174 billion was donated to the nation's nonprofits and charities in 1998 alone. That figure is indeed staggering. It almost appears as if a simple letter request to a charitable foundation or corporation would just bring in a flood of cash. Not so. In my experience an applicant *might* receive one grant for every 100 he or she applies for. Thus the need for the "development" of potential donors becomes critical.

A library manager might ask, "How would I have time to do anything else if I put all my energies into development?" Quite frankly, you wouldn't have any time to do anything else, let alone run your library. Development is a delicate balancing act for most library managers. After all, you do have other tasks to accomplish.

In a large library system, one has the option of creating a development department whose only task is to raise money for the library. This is a luxury in times of short staffing and limited funding opportunities. Still, there are a number of success stories in the field where a strong development department created not only a strong alternative funding stream but even an endowment for the library, funds from which could be used to support impressive institution-wide special programs (e.g., The New York Public Library). While it is imperative for the development department to have its share of staff with library experience, it is equally important to hire specialists whose expertise lies in the area of nonprofit development.

Developing a base of private donors takes time, effort, and knowledge of the tools and application processes and timetables. Grant writing is as much of a specialized skill as any other form of writing. The development staff must be well versed in the art of grant writing. New buzzwords enter the parlance regularly, and the style of writing that is expected in applications must be known by the grant writers so that they can properly apply for the funding available.

In the example of a small to medium-sized library, the task of development will fall to the director and perhaps a small cadre of carefully chosen staff. In such instances, the education process for staff drawn from the ranks must inevitably be a short one. However, there are a number of supportive tools one may employ in the search process. The first tool is to consult that great institution, The Foundation Center, in an effort to shorten the distance between the proposal and the check. The bibliography contains a number of resources published by The Foundation Center, all of which are designed to provide the sources to library managers to shortcut the process of applying for library project funding.

There are, as always, a number of opportunities for the development of local individuals, businesses, municipal, and statewide resources. Federal funding opportunities may be investigated through such agencies as the following:

- Institute for Museum and Library Services (IMLS) (www.imls. gov), ". . . an independent federal agency that fosters leadership, innovation and a lifetime of learning . . . supports all types of libraries and archives, from public to academic to research and school"[1] through LSTA grants administered by state libraries and National Leadership grants administered through IMLS.
- National Telecommunications and Information Administration (NTIA) (www.ntia.doc.gov), an agency of the U.S. Department of Commerce that offers funding under the Public Telecommunications Facilities Program (PTFP).
- National Endowment for the Humanities (NEH) (www.neh.gov), ". . . an independent grant-making agency of the U. S. government dedicated to supporting research, education and public programs in the humanities."[2]

In terms of corporate and family foundation funding, The Foundation Center offers the research and potential resources the library manager needs to consult in order to investigate this avenue of developmental approach. Searches of their databases can be specific and targeted to uncover sources appropriate to one's project, and their listing of sources is the most comprehensive available.

Gone are the days when the library could exist solely on the good graces of the tax money gleaned from the local municipality or school district. The library, although a nonprofit institution and a public service, can no longer operate as if it only has access to such funds. As funding streams ebb and flow, libraries must not remain locked into their bottom line. They must retain the ability to add to those resources as additional programs and services are expected to be available. As previously mentioned, funding has essentially dried up in terms of most donors' willingness to provide operating expenses to libraries. Basic organizational support is expected to be provided through municipal means only. Support for new programs and services will undoubtedly be easier to obtain. Most potential donors seek to fund new programs. Successful development, then, lies in the library's ability to reinvent itself. It must recreate its existing program and service base and repackage it as exciting new support opportunities for potential donors. The secret to successful development lies in a library's ability to make everything old seem new again. What does this mean?

For example, every library possesses unique qualities, perhaps its unusual building, one of its special collections, or even a program or service that means a great deal to the community. This uniqueness can certainly be presented to a potential donor in terms of its special qualities, its ability to serve the community in a manner that no other collection, program, or service can offer. These qualities can be packaged as "special purpose" items and funding can be requested on such a basis.

Some practical examples:

- The library needs new shelving for its compact disk collection. It also houses a rather extensive collection of vinyl records for which, although circulation has remained flat, there is still a solid core of borrowers. The library can appeal to either a corporate entity with a history of charitable funding for small library projects or small family foundations in order to arrange funding to purchase shelving for these collections. By doing this, not only does the vinyl find a home, but the compact disks can now be displayed in new, attractive housing built specifically for the disks.
- The library's local history collection may be emphasized for its importance to the community. The material is only available in print format and is severely deteriorating. It is imperative for the material to be transferred to an electronic format. Microfilming and/or digitization is expensive but necessary if the material is to survive. Funding may be sought to preserve the material, thus saving it for the good of the community.
- A number of libraries have offered potential donors "naming" possibilities. If libraries have stacks, then they also possess naming potential. For example, donors can have their name placed on a stack end and, in effect, sponsor that entire row of stacks. Individuals who lend their name to a stack end for a price do take pride in entering the library to show off their "stack plaque" to relatives and friends. For a library with a great many stacks, this can prove a development boom and a generous financial shot in the arm.
- The library building itself can offer the greatest development opportunity. If the building's historical value is significant because of its age, location, architecture, or its association with lit-

erary figures, there is always ample opportunity to exploit that connection.

- The community room of the library can serve as a place to hold various arts-related events for which a nominal fee can be charged. In order to create a funding stream in this area, the key is not to expend any library funds when holding an event. This also offers the possibility that others in attendance will recognize the value of the library's space for other social or arts-related rentals.

- There are local artists in every community who would be thrilled to have their works exhibited in a public space with so much foot traffic as the library. If works exhibited in the library are sold, the library can contract with the artist for a certain percentage of sales to go to the library.

- The library can benefit from its friends group by requesting that they develop a plan to fund some special program or service. As many successful museums around the world have done, the library may inform prospective members of the friends group that they are expected to donate a certain amount of money to the library to be spent specifically on needed programs and services. This can and should be written into the friend's group charter so that the mission is clear and the goals established in the document coincide with the goals of the library. Also, a fee structure ought to be established so that there are levels of friends based on the dues one can afford to pay. To accomplish successful development projects through the friends group, there must be more than a monetary incentive. Members of the friends must take into account the kind of work necessary to raise funds for the library. That is, when there are projects to be planned, volunteers must come forward so that the projects have a fighting chance of success (the library cannot have a bake sale without baked goods, a book sale without strong backs willing to haul the books to the sale tables, a special children's program without contacting parents, etc.).

As new funding streams are investigated by the library manager, he or she will come to recognize what works and what does not. The goal of these new funding streams is to increase the number of programs and services the library can provide, thus increasing the visibility of the library. Potential donors are more apt to offer matching or additional funding to a library with a strong development program. The successful development program is one that utilizes the additional dollars to offer the public more of what is expected. If it is more they want, it is more they should have.

Development funding can come from anywhere: individuals, corporations, family foundations, or the local, state, and federal government. Prospecting for development money to fund specific programs or services can lead the library manager to many potential sources. Therefore, a basic knowledge of where to look will start (as mentioned earlier) at The Foundation Center and proceed from there. The library manager may seek guidance from the selected list of Web resources listed here:

ALA OITP E-Rate Info
<http://www.ala.org/oitp>

The ALA Office for Information Technology Policy (OITP) and the ALA E-Rate Task Force have recently introduced a series of new Web pages concerning the E-Rate Year Four Program on the OITP Web site to assist all eligible libraries in applying for the E-Rate program. E-Rate is a federally funded program that provides affordable access to telecommunications services for schools and libraries, especially those located in economically depressed areas. The new OITP E-Rate Year Four Web pages highlight news regarding the E-rate program for all funding years, give useful hints concerning the forms and application process, and provide helpful links to the SLD and other Web sites. The Web pages also include contact information for the state E-Rate Coordinators for libraries, people in each state who help E-Rate applicants. The Task Force and the Coordinators also share development tools, resources such as templates, tracking forms, and Web site links to help reduce the complexity of the application process. Additionally, the SLD recently made available an EZ Filing Guide to assist in filing the E-Rate application. This form is available at: <http://www.sl.universalservice.org/reference/y4ez470guide.asp>. A link to the guide is also provided on the OITP Web site/E-Rate pages.

ALA Public Programs Office
Grants for Public Libraries
<http://www.ala.org/publicprograms/grants.html>

ALA/Information Today Inc. Library of the Future Award
<http://www.ala.org/work/awards/appls/lofappl.html>
The Information Today Library of the Future Award honors a library, library consortium, group of librarians, or support organization for innovative planning, applications, or development of patron training programs about information technology in a library setting. Criteria should include the benefit to clients served; benefit to the technology information community; impact on library operations; public relations value; and the impact on the perception of the library or librarian in the work setting and to the specialized or general public.

All About E-Rate
<http://www.intel.com/education/erate/INDEX.HTM>
A compilation of information by Intel. Describes the E-Rate, the application process, using E-Rate to build networks, and links to additional resources. Listed under Libraries.

Bill and Melinda Gates Foundation
<http://www.gatesfoundation.org/>
This U.S. library program makes grants to public libraries for the purpose of purchasing computers and hardware to bring Internet access to their patrons. As part of the grant, libraries also receive free training and technical assistance and other support, as well as donated software from Microsoft Corporation. The five-year goal of the library program is to provide grants to the more than 11,000 libraries in the United States and Canada serving low-income communities; provide training to librarians; and ensure information access for future generations. Listed under Libraries.

FCC Releases New FAQ on Universal Service
<http://www.fcc.gov/Bureaus/Common_Carrier/Public_Notices/1997/da971374.html>
Important notice for libraries and public schools looking for assistance in acquiring access to the World Wide Web. The Federal Communications Commission has released "Frequently Asked Questions

on Universal Service and the Snowe-Rockefeller Amendment." The document responds to forty questions on the libraries and schools portion of the Universal Service Order that was adopted on May 7, 1997. Categories of the FAQ include: Eligibility for Universal Service Discounts, Services and Functionalities Eligible for Discounts, Discounts, Funding, Restrictions Imposed on Schools and Libraries, and Applying for Discounts and Implementation. The FAQ is also available online from the FCC Universal Service page at <http://www.fcc.gov.ccb/universal_service/>. Listed under Education; Libraries.

Funding and Grant Resources for Libraries and Librarians
<http://www.libraryhq.com/funding.html>
Links provided by LibraryHQ.Com.

Library Services and Technology Act (LSTA) Funding Web Site
The American Library Association (ALA) (sponsors) a Web site and electronic brochure devoted to helping ensure the reauthorization of the Library Services and Technology Act (LSTA). LSTA is the only federal legislation that funds libraries exclusively. The LSTA coalition comprises a range of ALA division members and representatives from Chief Officers of State Library Agencies (COSLA), the Regional OCLC Network Directors Advisory Council, and observers from the National Commission on Library and Information Services (NCLIS) and Institute of Museum and Library Services (IMLS). The electronic brochure is designed to be downloaded by librarians and disseminated to their patrons. The brochure resides on a new Web page dedicated to LSTA, located at <www.ala.org/washoff/lsta.html>. The Web site includes contact information for reaching state LSTA coordinators, a toolkit for advocating on this vital legislation, and an opportunity to share LSTA library success stories.[3]

Northeast Documents Preservation Center: Funding Sources
<http://www.nedcc.org/funding.htm>
Brief descriptions of grant programs that provide funding for the preservation of paper-based collections in libraries, archives, museums, historical societies, and public agencies.

Schools and Libraries Corporation
<http://www.sl.universalservice.org/>

The Schools and Libraries Division (SLD) of the Universal Service Administrative Company (USAC) provides affordable access to telecommunications services for all eligible schools and libraries in the United States. The program provides discounts on telecommunications services, Internet access, and internal connections. For more information about other universal service programs, click on: <http://www.universalservice.org>. Listed under Education; Libraries.

Web Resources for Tribal Libraries
<http://www.u.arizona.edu/~ecubbins/index.html>

This site provides links to potential funding sources for North American Indian tribal libraries. A tribal library may be public, academic, school, or special, such as an archive or museum.

Chapter 11

A Dynamic Dozen:
Management Classics
for the Twenty-First Century
Library Manager

The following is a carefully selected annotated bibliography of management "classics" that offer the rare combination of intelligence, relevance, psychology, philosophy, and practical good sense in today's library environment. This selection is a wholly personal one. But since there are literally tens of thousands of management and related titles in print, with more being published each day, it would be impossible to analyze the value of them all. Nor are a great number of them worth extensive analysis.

In titles presented here, one may find certain constants. Their value lies in the fact that they can be used as a reference library for today's manager. They are to be frequently consulted to provide a support mechanism a manager can rely on to effectively offer the appropriate level of wisdom. By doing so, the manager can then guide the library with not only an equal dose of knowledge and intelligence, but a strong sense of humanity toward their colleagues.

This is not, by any means, a traditional bibliography. For example, the reader will notice that the *I Ching* is included in this list. I have been asked, "How do we bring staff along so that they accept the change that is occurring in our organization?" The *I Ching* provides the answer within its philosophy. If one accepts change and allows it to become the norm, a certain calmness and understanding can develop and create a less upsetting work environment.

Another seeming anomaly, the reader will notice Daniel P. Goleman's *Emotional Intelligence* included on the list. While his later work has dealt specifically with the workplace, this groundbreaking book centers on the strength of one's emotional intelligence rather than IQ and analyzes its importance for managers.

The books have not been awarded any particular numerical ranking. One may favor a specific title over another. However, if a library manager, either new to the field or seasoned through years of experience, has not yet read any of them, I suggest reading them at least once through armed with a highlighter and notepad in hand so that he or she may consult these experts as needed.

1. *The One Minute Manager* by D. Kenneth Blanchard, Spencer Johnson, and Kenneth H. Blanchard

The granddaddy of them all. First published in 1982, this work ranks with such slim publications as *The Communist Manifesto* and *The Prince* as a small book with tremendous impact. This book was, and remains, a phenomenon. It is practical and, while seemingly simplistic in nature, may be likened to a Zen parable or a self-discovery book published later (such as *The Celestine Prophecy*) wherein the reader follows a young man in search of greater insight. In this case, the holy grail he seeks is the management skill he requires to obtain the most productivity from the people who work for him. This book combines everyday wisdom with real-world goals and is an indispensable tool for the manager who also pursues the objective of becoming a respected leader. Today, the book is often provided to a company's fresh-faced new executives on the day they report to work to be used as a standard management instrument. They are encouraged to learn it inside and out as a ready-reference tool to be placed in their bag of management tricks. They are motivated not only to read it, but to refer to it regularly in making management decisions.

2. *The 3 Keys to Empowerment: Release the Power Within People for Astonishing Results* by Kenneth H. Blanchard, John Carlos, Alan Randolph, and Ken Blanchard

The authors successfully cooperate to transcend the drawbacks of using a word that has been more than abused in the language of management-speak. They are able to overcome the clichés of "empowerment" and provide important steps to opening up the decision-making process as a group effort. A good idea can come from anywhere or anyone, and this work provides the manager with the tools to establish the means by which the free flow of thoughts and ideas can flourish in an open environment. The authors explain that the "three keys" include "information" which should be generously shared, establishing "clear parameters" that can be understood by all, and explaining the value of "team building" in order to include all members of the team in the empowerment process. The book is especially essential for library managers whose libraries are in a transitional period from offering little or no technology to offering a product primarily through technological means.

3. *In Search of Excellence* by Thomas J. Peters and Robert H. Waterman, Jr.

The authors of this book, considered the bible of American management, studied several dozen companies to uncover their secrets to success. Eight basic management principles are expounded upon along with numerous examples of how those principles can be employed to the organization's best advantage. This book focuses on the similarities among successful companies. Regardless of the industry, the eight basic principles can be applied equally. Although this is another work published in the early 1980s, the principles are as relevant today as ever.

4. *Emotional Intelligence* by Daniel P. Goleman

This book offers a thoughtful assessment of the role of IQ and the way that we value it over "emotional intelligence," which, the author argues, is much more important in creating a well-rounded, functioning human being. We require more than simply high intelligence to be successful in business and in life. We must be encouraged to allow our emotional intelligence to flower in a society that must learn to value not only intelligence but emotion-rich individuals who can provide better leadership on the job and engage in more successful personal relationships at home. Each section of the book is peppered with analogies to support Goleman's argument. One comes away from this book convinced that we must shift our thinking in terms of the author's argument in order to structure a flourishing social and business environment.

5. *The Fifth Discipline* by Peter M. Senge

What used to be called problems are now called challenges. When an organization has a challenge to face, there is no better book to be consulted than this one. Senge places the responsibility for overcoming challenges squarely upon the shoulders of the entire organization, which must go through a learning curve in order to meet them. Like individuals, organizations, too, can suffer the effects of a learning disability. If this is the case, its employees may elect to master Senge's five disciplines to overcome and persevere. His innovative approach to corporate learning is built on thinking, personal mastery of various skills, "mental models," "the deeply ingrained assumptions . . ." that influence learning, and finally building a shared vision and team learning based on dialogue. Not only does the author write with authority and sensitivity, a rare combination in business primers, but he is able to round out the discussion of these disciplines with a combination of spirituality and psychological analysis that is both easily readable and supremely intelligent.

6. *Thriving on Chaos: Handbook for a Management Revolution* by Tom Peters

One the richest texts on the subject available. It includes a section titled "Learning to Love Change," a philosophy more in tune with the *I Ching* than any other management text. The positive reinforcement continues throughout the book, and even the section on "empowering" people is written with no trace of condescension. Well-worn words such as "vision," "decentralize," "revamp," "reconceive," and so many others take on a clear and definite urgency in this book. The word "heroes" is used to further empower staffers to envision themselves in that role and to urge them to take part in the creation of an environment where one does not have to "swim with sharks," or become one, to survive change in the organization.

7. *Further Up the Organization* by Robert Townsend

This 1984 follow-up to Townsend's 1970 masterwork, *Up the Organization,* is a call to arms to those who aim to create an organization that exists to best serve its staff. He encourages workers to become guerrilla warriors in the battle against corporate complacency. The book is extremely user friendly, and the chapters are even laid out in alphabetical order for easy reference. It is probably the most humorous of all the books on this list. Townsend's sly, smart, and slightly cynical view of what needs to be done to reinvent the organization is entertaining as well as educational.

8. *Teaching the Elephant to Dance: Empowering Change in Your Corporation* by James A. Belasco

How can a manager implement change and further his or her vision in an atmosphere of strident reluctance? Of course, there is that word again: "empowerment." Given the tone of this book, one of mild panic, it appears to have been written in 1990 as a direct result of the numerous foreign takeovers that left Americans wondering if we had lost our edge along with our assets. His watchwords are "change or die!" Melodramatic, perhaps, but such a wake-up call was necessary in the author's opinion. The layout of the book is very straightforward, more like a technical manual than a pseudoentertainment like the previous listing. He begins the book explaining exactly why change is necessary for survival and by the final chapter convinces the reader in a step-by-step process how change can be accomplished. He cannot emphasize enough the fact that if a company is slow to change, it will be left behind, and then so will America. American companies, he states, must be "fleet of foot," and it is the managers who will take their companies into the next millennium. It is their "duty" to effect change, to make the elephant dance, and those who do not are not deserving of the title "manager."

9. *A Passion for Excellence: The Leadership Difference* by Tom Peters, Nancy K. Austin, and Thomas J. Peters

The key element in this work is the word "passion." Mr. Peters clearly maintains a passion for both customers and employees, the two groups that make a company responsive, successful, and able to transform itself into whatever is expected of it in the marketplace. The book breaks down into a personal look at a number of companies to discover what makes them successful. How do managers keep passion alive so that a company is inspired to excellence? Through four basic elements: continuous innovation, staying in touch and listening to your customers, encouragement of the staff, and exhibiting integrity that inspires great leadership. The passionate nature of the individual can be inspired to do great things in business as in life. When passion takes over, the pure joy in leading a group of individuals to create a decision that affects the customer will awaken even a dormant workplace.

10. *Transforming the Organization* by James N. Kelly and Francis Gouillart

The authors were hired as consultants by some of the largest global entities to assist them in transforming into powerhouses ready to face the constant inevitable changes in the modern marketplace. Through a series of case histories, Kelly and Gouillart examine the patient (the company) and determine its illness, and then are able to prescribe the proper medicine, not just to cure it, but to allow it to prosper.

The philosophy of corporate transformation as a constant is as important as defining the company's mission and vision. It is the means by which a company can gain an edge ensuring future successful growth. In its way, it takes the philosophy of change as norm and bends it slightly to its own devices. Perhaps it is a less radical concept than it first appeared to be when it was published. It literally takes the old cliché "treat the disease, not the patient" to a comprehensible level.

11. *The Frontiers of Management: Where Tomorrow's Decisions Are Being Shaped Today* by Peter Ferdinand Drucker

No listing of this sort would be complete without this seminal work by Peter Drucker, management's chief tutor. Unquestionably the single most influential expert in the field, he maintains that to a manager, "change is opportunity." In the modern world, these opportunities present themselves at such a rate of speed that they are easy to miss; thus the manager must be prepared and armed with the essential tools to make the most of them. A philosopher as much as a journalist, Professor Drucker has created a book that deals with not only the impending changes in world economies, but how businesses and their employees and customers will be affected by these tremendous changes. He is a genius at expounding on the future direction of the global economy and has always been way ahead of his time in his accurate forecasts. He also examines the plight of the manager whose career might have hit a plateau while change happens in the company and offers advice on what can be done to elevate him or her above that plateau. He offers a volume of real-world philosophy and practical advice, a combination that has been applauded for decades.

12. The *I Ching* (Book of Changes)

Why do I include the oldest surviving text in Chinese culture in this list of management classics? After reading through the previous entries, it is probably self-evident at this point. The commonality of all the preceding texts is their basic thesis that managers must use, as their source of inspiration, change. The *I Ching* is to the Chinese, life, breath, our spiritual existence, and the recognition that, as Confucius has written, "Everything flows on and on like this river, without pause, day and night." In all of the other texts listed, the commonality lies in a sense of urgency. The authors impart the knowledge that we are obligated to change, to recognize that life does not stand still, and that the best managers are those who perceive this and impart that knowledge to their staff. Finally, like these texts, The *I Ching* provides its adherents with the tools by which to act and react to the continual change found in our lives, and although it is a 3,000-year-old text, its lessons are as useful today as ever. Of course, there are Eastern subtleties in the text that can never properly be transliterated into Western culture. However, it remains a book for the ages, a book to keep on the shelf next to the others and consulted regularly for its timeless wisdom.

Appendix A

ALA-Accredited Library Schools

Alabama

The University of Alabama
School of Library and Information Studies
Box 870252
Tuscaloosa, AL 35487-0252
Phone: 205-348-4610
Fax: 205-348-3746
<www.slis.ua.edu>

• Master of Library and Information Studies

Other degrees or certificates:

• PhD, Library and Information Studies
• Educational Specialist in Library and Information Studies
• Master of Fine Arts, Book Arts

Distance education opportunities:

• Birmingham, Gadsden, Huntsville, Mobile, AL

Arizona

University of Arizona
School of Information Resources and Library Science
1515 East First Street
Tucson, AZ 85719
Phone: 520-621-3565
Fax: 520-621-3279
sirls@u.arizona.edu

Degrees accredited by the American Library Association:

- Master of Arts

Other degrees or certificates:

- PhD

Distance education opportunities:

- Internet

California

San Jose State University
School of Library and Information Science
One Washington Square
San Jose, CA 95192-0029
Phone: 408-924-2490
Fax: 408-924-2476
office@wahoo.sjsu.edu
<slisweb.sjsu.edu>

- Master of Library and Information Science

Distance education opportunities:

- Fullerton, Northridge, Palm Springs, Pasadena, Sacramento, San Diego, San Francisco, San Marcos, Sonoma, CA
- Two-way interactive video
- Web supported

University of California, Los Angeles
Department of Information Studies
Graduate School of Education and Information Studies
2320 Moore Hall
Mailbox 951521
Los Angeles, CA 90095-1521
Phone: 310-825-8799
Fax: 310-206-3076
Admissions
Phone: 310-825-5269

Fax: 310-206-6293
<http://is.gseis.ucla.edu>

- Master of Library and Information Science

Other degrees or certificates:

- PhD
- Post-MLIS
- MLIS/MA, History
- MLIS/MA, Latin American Studies
- MLIS/MBA

Connecticut

Southern Connecticut State University
School of Communication, Information and Library Science
Department of Library Science and Instructional Technology
501 Crescent Street
New Haven, CT 06515
Phone: 203-392-5781 or toll-free 1-888-500-7278, press 4
Fax: 203-392-5780
<www.southernct.edu/departments/ils>

- Master of Library Science

Other degrees or certificates:

- MLS/JD
- MLS/MS, Chemistry
- MLS/MS, English
- MLS/MS, Foreign Languages
- MLS/MS, History
- MS, Instructional Technology
- MS, Instructional Technology/MS, Chemistry
- MS, Instructional Technology/MS, History
- Sixth Year Diploma in Library Information Studies
- School Media Specialist certification

Distance education opportunities:

- Online

District of Columbia

The Catholic University of America
School of Library and Information Science
Washington, DC 20064
Phone: 202-319-5085
Fax: 202-319-5574
cua-slis@cua.edu

- Master of Science in Library Science

Other degrees or certificates:

- MSLS/JD
- MSLS/MA, English
- MSLS/MA, Greek and Latin
- MSLS/MA, History
- MSLS/MA, Musicology
- MSLS/MA, Religious Studies
- MSLS/MS, Biology
- Post-Masters Certificate

Distance education opportunities:

- Fairfax, Norfolk, Richmond, VA

Florida

Florida State University
School of Information Studies
Tallahassee, FL 32306-2100
Phone: 850-644-5775
Fax: 850-644-9763
<www.lis.fsu.edu>

- Master of Science
- Master of Arts

Other degrees or certificates:

- PhD
- Specialist
- BS, Information Studies

- School Media Certification
- Certificate in Museum Studies and Information Studies
- BS, International Studies

Distance education opportunities:

- Internet

University of South Florida
School of Library and Information Science
4202 East Fowler Avenue, CIS 1040
Tampa, FL 33620-7800
Phone: 813-974-3520
Fax: 813-974-6840
<www.cas.usf.edu/lis/>

- Master of Arts

Other degrees or certificates:

- Educational Media Certification

Distance education opportunities:

- Ft. Lauderdale, Ft. Myers, Gainesville, Lakeland, Miami, Orlando, Palm Beach, Sarasota, FL
- Internet

Georgia

Clark Atlanta University
School of Library and Information Studies
300 Trevor Arnett Hall
223 James P. Brawley Drive
Atlanta, GA 30314
Phone: 404-880-8697
Fax: 404-880-8977
<www.cau.edu>

- Master of Science in Library Service

Other degrees or certificates:

- Specialist in Library Service
- State of Georgia Certification for School Media Center Services

Hawaii

University of Hawaii
Library and Information Science Program
2550 The Mall
Honolulu, HI 96822
Phone: 808-956-7321
Fax: 808-956-5835
<www.hawaii.edu/slis/>

- Master of Library and Information Science

Other degrees or certificates:

- PhD, Interdisciplinary Program in Communications and Information Sciences
- Certificate in Advanced Library and Information Science

Distance education opportunities:

- Hawaii Interactive Television System (HITS) limited to islands of Hawaii, Kauai, Lanai, Maui, Molokai, and Oahu (six sites)

Illinois

Dominican University
Graduate School of Library and Information Science
7900 West Division Street
River Forest, IL 60305
Phone: 708-524-6845
Fax: 708-524-6657
gslis@email.dom.edu
<www.dom.edu/academic/gslishome.html>
<www.stkate.edu> (College of St. Catherine)

- Master of Library and Information Science

Other degrees or certificates:

- MLIS/MA, Public History
- MLIS/MBA
- MLIS/Master of Divinity
- MLIS/Master of Music, Music History

- MS, Management Information Systems
- Certificate of Special Studies in Law Librarianship
- Certificate of Special Studies in Library Administration
- Certificate of Special Studies in Technical Services
- Illinois Standard Special Certificate in Media Specialist (K-12)
- BA/MLIS

Distance education opportunities:

- Chicago, Northbrook, Vernon Hills, IL; St. Paul, MN

University of Illinois at Urbana-Champaign
Graduate School of Library and Information Science
Library and Information Science Building
501 East Daniel Street
Champaign, IL 61820
Phone: 217-333-3280
Fax: 217-244-3302
<alexia.lis.uiuc.edu>

- Master of Science

Other degrees or certificates:

- PhD
- Certificate of Advanced Study
- Undergraduate Minor in Information Studies

Distance education opportunities:

- Internet

Indiana

Indiana University
School of Library and Information Science
Main Library 011
1320 E. 10th Street
Bloomington, IN 47405-3907
Phone: 812-855-2018
Fax: 812-855-6166
slis@indiana.edu

- Master of Information Science
- Master of Library Science

Other degrees or certificates:

- PhD, Information Science
- MIS/MPI, Master of Planning
- MIS/MPA, Master of Public Affairs
- MIS/MA, Russian and East European Studies
- MLS/JD
- MLS/MA, Comparative Literature
- MLS/MA, History
- MLS/MA, Art History
- MLS/MA, History and Philosophy of Science
- MLS/MA, Journalism
- MLS/MA, Latin American and Carribean Studies
- MLS/MA, Music (Musicology or Music Theory)
- MLS/MA, Russian and East European Studies
- MLS/MPS, Master of Public Affairs
- Public Library Certification
- School Library Media and Information Technology Certification

Iowa

University of Iowa
School of Library and Information Science
3087 Library
Iowa City, IA 52242-1420
Phone: 319-335-5707
Fax: 319-335-5374
<www.uiowa.edu/~libsci>

- Master of Arts

Other degrees or certificates:

- MA/JD
- MA/MBA

Distance education opportunities:

- Various sites within Iowa

Kansas

Emporia State University
School of Library and Information Management
PO Box 4025
Emporia, KS 66801
Phone: 316-341-5203
Fax: 316-341-5233
<slim.emporia.edu>

- Master of Library Science

Other degrees or certificates:

- PhD, Library and Information Management
- MLS/History, English, Music, and Business
- School Library Media Specialist
- Information Management Certification
- BS, Information Resource Studies (interdisciplinary)

Distance education opportunities:

- Denver, CO; Overland Park, KS; Albuquerque, NM; Portland, OR; Salt Lake City, UT
- Videotape, interactive video, Internet

Kentucky

University of Kentucky
College of Communications and Information Studies
School of Library and Information Science
502 King Library Building S
Lexington, KY 40506-0039
Phone: 859-257-8876
Fax: 859-257-4205
<www.uky.edu/CommInfoStudies/SLIS/>

- Master of Arts
- Master of Science in Library Science

Other degrees or certificates:

- PhD
- LIS, tract in Communication

Distance education opportunities:

- Covington, Elizabethtown, Highland Heights, Louisville, KY; Cincinnati, OH
- Interactive video, Internet

Louisiana

Louisiana State University
School of Library and Information Science
267 Coates Hall
Baton Rouge, LA 70803
Phone: 225-578-3158
Fax: 225-578-4581
slis@lsu.edu
<http://slis.lsu.edu>

- Master of Library and Information Science

Other degrees or certificates:

- MLIS/MA, History
- MLIS/MS, Systems Science
- Certificate of Advanced Study in Library and Information Science
- Certification in School Librarianship for the State of Louisiana

Distance education opportunities:

- Alexandria, Eunice, Lake Charles, Monroe, New Orleans, Shreveport, LA
- Two-way interactive video, Internet (selected courses)

Maryland

University of Maryland
College of Information Studies
4105 Hornbake Library Building
College Park, MD 20742-4345
Phone: 301-405-2033
Fax: 301-314-9145
<www.clis.umd.edu>

- Master of Library Science

Other degrees or certificates:

- PhD, Library and Information Science
- MLS/GeLS, Geography
- MLS/HiLS, History

Massachusetts

Simmons College
Graduate School of Library and Information Science
300 The Fenway
Boston, MA 02115-5898
Phone: 617-521-2800
Fax: 617-521-3192
gslis@simmons.edu
<www.simmons.edu/programs/gslis>

- Master of Science

Other degrees or certificates:

- DA
- MS/MA, History
- MS/MA, Education

Michigan

University of Michigan
School of Information
304 West Hall Building
550 East University Avenue
Ann Arbor, MI 48109-1092
Phone: 734-763-2285
Fax: 734-764-2475
si.admissions@umich.edu
<www.si.umich.edu>

- Master of Science in Information

Other degrees or certificates:

- MSI/MSN, Nursing
- MSI/MBA, Business Administration
- MSI/JD, Law
- MSI/MPP, Public Policy

Wayne State University
Library and Information Science Program
106 Kresge Library
Detroit, MI 48202
Phone: 313-577-1825
Fax: 313-577-7563
<www.lisp.wayne.edu>

- Master of Library and Information Science

Other degrees or certificates:

- Specialist certificate
- Archival Administration certificate

Distance education opportunities:

- Farmington, Flint, Grand Rapids, Kalamazoo, Lansing, Saginaw, MI

Mississippi

University of Southern Mississippi
School of Library and Information Science
Box 5146
Hattiesburg, MS 39406-5146
Phone: 601-266-4228
Fax: 601-266-5774
<www-dept.usm.edu/~slis>

- Master of Library and Information Science

Other degrees or certificates:

- MLIS/MA, Anthropology
- MLIS/MA, History
- MLIS with School Library Media Licensure
- Specialist in Library and Information Science
- BA with Major in Library and Information Science
- BA in LIS with School Library Media Licensure

Distance education opportunities:

- Online, interactive video

Missouri

University of Missouri–Columbia
School of Information Science and Learning Technologies
303 Townsend Hall
Columbia, MO 65211
Phone: 573-882-4546
Fax: 573-884-2917
<www.coe.missouri.edu/~sislt>

- Master of Arts (2004)

Distance education opportunities:

- Kansas City, Springfield, St. Louis, MO
- Internet

New Jersey

Rutgers University
School of Communication, Information and Library Studies
4 Huntington Street
New Brunswick, NJ 08901-1071
Phone: 732-932-7917
Fax: 732-932-2644
scilsmls@scils.rutgers.edu
<www.scils.rutgers.edu>

- Master of Library Service

Other degrees or certificates:

- PhD, Communication, Information and Library Studies
- Sixth-Year Specialist Program

New York

Long Island University
Palmer School of Library and Information Science
C. W. Post Campus
720 Northern Boulevard
Brookville, NY 11548-1300

Phone: 516-299-2866
Fax: 516-299-4168
palmer@cwpost.liu.edu
<http://palmer.cwpost.liu.edu>

- Master of Science in Library and Information Science

Other degrees or certificates:

- PhD, Information Studies
- BS, Information Transfer
- Certificate in Archives and Records Management

Distance education opportunities:

- Manhattan, Westchester County, NY

Pratt Institute
School of Information and Library Science
Information Science Center
200 Willoughby Avenue
Brooklyn, NY 11205
Phone: 718-636-3702
Fax: 718-636-3733
infosils@pratt.edu
<http://www.pratt.edu/sils>

- Master of Science in Library and Information Science

Other degrees or certificates:

- MS/JD
- MSLIS/MS, Art History
- Advanced Certificate

Queens College
City University of New York
Graduate School of Library and Information Studies
65-30 Kissena Boulevard
Flushing, NY 11367
Phone: 718-997-3790
Fax: 718-997-3797

gslis@qcunixl.qc.edu
<www.qc.edu/GSLIS/>

- Master of Library Science (2004)

Other degrees or certificates:

- Post-Masters Certificate Program

St. John's University
Division of Library and Information Science
8000 Utopia Parkway
Jamaica, NY 11439
Phone: 718-990-6200
Fax: 718-990-2071
libis@stjohns.edu
<www.stjohns.edu/pls/portal30/sjudev.school.home?p_siteid=38&p_
   navbars=249&p_id=50623>

- Master of Library Science

Other degrees or certificates:

- MLS/MA, Government and Politics
- MLS/MS, Pharmaceutical Sciences
- Advanced Certificate in Library and Information Studies

Syracuse University
School of Information Studies
4-206 Center for Science and Technology
Syracuse, NY 13244-4100
Phone: 315-443-2911
Fax: 315-443-5806
<istweb.syr.edu>

- Master of Library Science

Other degrees or certificates:

- PhD in Information Transfer
- MS, Information Resources Management
- MS, Telecommunications and Network Management
- BS, Information Management and Technology
- Certificate in Telecommunications and Network Management

Distance education opportunities:

- Washington, DC (MS, Information Resources Management); Toronto (MS, Telecommunications and Network Management)
- Short 1 week residencies for core courses on Syracuse University Campus with Internet-based home study for course assignment completion

University at Albany
State University of New York
School of Information Science and Policy
135 Western Avenue
Draper 113
Albany, NY 12222
Phone: 518-442-5110
Fax: 518-442-5367
infosci@albany.edu
<www.albany.edu/sisp/>

- Master of Library Science

Other degrees or certificates:

- PhD, Information Science (Interdisciplinary Program)
- MLS/MA, English
- MLS/MA, History
- MSIS
- Certificate of Advanced Study

Distance education opportunities:

- New Paltz, Poughkeepsie, NY

University at Buffalo
State University of New York
School of Informatics
Department of Library and Information Studies
534 Baldy Hall
North Campus
Buffalo, NY 14260-1020
Phone: 716-645-2412
Fax: 716-645-3775

UB-LIS@buffalo.edu
<www.informatics.buffalo.edu/lis>

- Master of Library Science

Other degrees or certificates:

- MIC, Master of Arts in Information and Communication
- MLS/JD, Legal Information Management and Analysis
- MLS/MA, Music History/Music Librarianship
- PhD, Communication with Cognate in Library and Information Studies
- Post-Master's Certificate

Distance education opportunities:

- Satellite: Rochester, NY (selected courses)
- Internet (selected courses)
- Two-way interactive video to Elmira, NY (selected courses)

North Carolina

North Carolina Central University
School of Library and Information Sciences
1801 Fayetteville St., PO Box 19586
Durham, NC 27707
Phone: 919-530-6485
Fax: 919-530-6402
<www.slis.nccu.edu>

- Master of Library Science

Other degrees or certificates:

- MLS/JD
- MIS
- MBA/MIS
- Media Coordinator Certificate

Distance education opportunities:

- Fayetteville, Greenville, Hickory, Pembroke, Wilmington, NC

University of North Carolina at Chapel Hill
School of Information and Library Science
CB #3360 100 Manning Hall
Chapel Hill, NC 27599-3360
Phone: 919-962-8366
Fax: 919-962-8071
info@ils.unc.edu
<www.ils.unc.edu>

- Master of Science in Library Science
- Master of Science in Information Science

Other degrees or certificates:

- PhD, Information and Library Science
- Certificate of Advanced Study

University of North Carolina at Greensboro
Department of Library and Information Studies
School of Education
P.O. Box 26171
Greensboro, NC 27402-6171
Phone: 336-334-3477
Fax: 336-334-5060
<www.uncg.edu/lis/>

- Master of Library and Information Studies

Other degrees or certificates:

- Media Coordinator Certificate
- Media Supervisor Certificate
- Instructional Technology Specialist, Computer

Distance education opportunities:

- Asheville, Charlotte, NC

Ohio

Kent State University
School of Library and Information Science
Room 314 Library
PO Box 5190

Kent, OH 44242-0001
Phone: 330-672-2782
Fax: 330-672-7965
<web.slis.kent.edu>

- Master of Library and Information Science

Other degrees or certificates:

- Certificate of Advanced Study in Library and Information Science
- Graduate New Media Certificate
- Information Architecture/Knowledge Management (IAKM)
- Undergraduate New Media Certificate

Distance education opportunities:

- Athens, Bowling Green (limited program on-site and via electronic distance learning), Cincinnati, Columbus (complete program on-site), OH

Oklahoma

University of Oklahoma
School of Library and Information Studies
401 West Brooks, Room 120
Norman, OK 73019-6032
Phone: 405-325-3921
Fax: 405-325-7648
slisinfo@lists.ou.edu
<www.ou.edu/cas/slis/>

- Master of Library and Information Studies

Other degrees or certificates:

- Bachelor of Arts in Information Studies
- MLIS/MA, History of Science
- MLIS/Master of Education
- Generic Dual Master's Degree
- Certificate of Advanced Studies

Distance education opportunities:

- Ardmore, Chickasha, Durant, Enid, Lawton, Tulsa, Weatherford, OK

Pennsylvania

Clarion University of Pennsylvania
Department of Library Science
840 Wood St.
Clarion, PA 16214-1232
Phone: 814-393-2271
Fax: 814-393-2150
<www.clarion.edu/libsci>

- Master of Science in Library Science

Other degrees or certificates:

- Certificate of Advanced Studies in Library Science
- BSEd Library Science

Distance education opportunities:

- Harrisburg, Southpointe, PA
- Interactive television

Drexel University
College of Information Science and Technology
3141 Chestnut Street
Philadelphia, PA 19104-2875
Phone: 215-895-2474
Fax: 215-895-2494
<www.cis.drexel.edu>

- Master of Science

Other degrees or certificates:

- PhD
- MSIS
- MSSE
- Certificate of Advanced Study
- Competitive Intelligence Certificate

Distance education opportunities:

- Internet

University of Pittsburgh
School of Information Sciences
505 IS Building
Pittsburgh, PA 15260
Phone: 412-624-5230
Fax: 412-624-5231
<www2.sis.pitt.edu>

- Master of Library and Information Science

Other degrees or certificates:

- PhD, Library and Information Science
- PhD, Information Science and Telecommunications
- PhD, Telecommunications
- CAS, Library and Information Science
- MSIS
- MST, Telecommunications
- BSIS

Puerto Rico

University of Puerto Rico
Graduate School of Information Sciences and Technologies
PO Box 21906
San Juan, PR 00931-1906
Phone: 787-763-6199
Fax: 787-764-2311
73253.312@compuserve.com

- Master of Library Science

Rhode Island

University of Rhode Island
Graduate School of Library and Information Studies
Rodman Hall
Kingston, RI 02881
Phone: 401-874-2947
Fax: 401-874-4964
gslis@etal.uri.edu
<www.uri.edu/artsci/lsc>

- Master of Library and Information Studies

Other degrees or certificates:

- MLIS/MA, History
- MLIS/MPA, Public Administration

Distance education opportunities:

- Amherst, Boston, MA; Durham, NH
- Internet, interactive video

South Carolina

University of South Carolina
College of Library and Information Science
Davis College
Columbia, SC 29208
Phone: 803-777-3858
Fax: 803-777-7938

- Master of Library and Information Science

Other degrees or certificates:

- MLIS, Applied History
- MLIS, English
- Certificate of Graduate Study in Library and Information Science

Distance education opportunities:

- Degree programs in selected states per contract arrangements

Tennessee

University of Tennessee
School of Information Sciences
804 Volunteer Boulevard
Knoxville, TN 37996-4330
Phone: 865-974-2148
Fax: 865-974-4967

- Master of Science

Other degrees and certificates:

- PhD in Communications with a primary concentration in Information Sciences
- School Librarianship Endorsement (TN)

Texas

Texas Woman's University
School of Library and Information Studies
PO Box 425438
Denton, TX 76204-5438
Phone: 940-898-2602
Fax: 940-898-2611
<www.libraryschool.net>

- Master of Library Science
- Master of Arts in Library Science

Other degrees or certificates:

- PhD
- Learning Resources Endorsement

Distance education opportunities:

- Dallas, TX
- Interactive video: Corpus Christi, Edinburg, Texarkana, Tyler (a cooperative with the University of North Texas)
- Internet (selected courses)

University of North Texas
School of Library and Information Sciences
PO Box 311068, NT Station
Denton, TX 76203-1068
Phone: 940-565-2445
Fax: 940-565-3101
slis@unt.edu
<www.unt.edu/slis/>

- Master of Science

Other degrees or certificates:

- PhD, Information Science (Interdisciplinary)
- MS/MA, History
- Certificate of Advanced Study
- School Librarianship/Learning Resources Endorsement
- Graduate Academic Certificate in Youth Services

Distance education opportunities:

- Houston, Lubbock, TX; Minneapolis, St. Cloud, MN
- Internet

The University of Texas at Austin
Graduate School of Library and Information Science
Austin, TX 78712-1276
Phone: 512-471-3821
Fax: 512-471-3971
info@gslis.utexas.edu
<www.gslis.utexas.edu>

- Master of Library and Information Science

Other degrees or certificates:

- PhD, Library and Information Science
- Certificate of Advanced Study
- Learning Resource Endorsement
- Endorsement of Specialization

Distance education opportunities:

- El Paso, San Antonio, TX
- Interactive television

Washington

University of Washington
The Information School
Mary Gates Hall, Suite 370
Box 352840
Seattle, WA 98195-2840
Phone: 206-543-1794

Fax: 206-616-3152
info@ischool.washington.edu
<www.ischool.washington.edu>

- Master of Library and Information Science

Other degrees or certificates:

- PhD, Information Science
- Data Resource Management Certificate
- Genealogy and Family History Certificate
- Information and Records Management Certificate
- School Library Media Certificate
- Special Certificate in Law Librarianship
- BS, Informatics

Distance education opportunities:

- Contact UW Extension Office
  Phone: 206-543-2320 or 206-685-6506

Wisconsin

University of Wisconsin–Madison
School of Library and Information Studies
Helen C. White Hall
600 North Park Street, Rm 4217
Madison, WI 53706
Phone: 608-263-2900
Fax: 608-263-4849
uw-slis@slis.wisc.edu
<www.slis.wisc.edu>

- Master of Arts

Other degrees or certificates:

- PhD
- Specialist Degree

Distance education opportunities:

- Noncredit continuing education via Educational Teleconferencing
  Network (ETN) and Web-based

University of Wisconsin–Milwaukee
School of Library and Information Science
Enderis Hall 1110
2400 East Hartford Avenue
Milwaukee, WI 53201
Phone: 414-229-4707
Fax: 414-229-4848
info@sois.uwm.edu
<www.sois.uwm.edu>

- Master of Library and Information Science

Other degrees or certificates:

- PhD (Multidisciplinary)
- MLIS/MA, Geography, History, English, Foreign Language and Literature
- MLIS/MM, Music
- MLIS/MS, Anthropology
- MLIS/MS, Urban Studies
- Certificate of Advanced Study
- BS, Information Resources

Distance education opportunities:

- Fox Valley, River Falls, WI; Satellite sites throughout the state of Wisconsin

Appendix B

Surveys

TECHNOLOGY NEEDS ASSESSMENT QUESTIONNAIRE
How to Fill Out This Survey

Select your skill-level ranking based on the **experience you have now.** Experience levels are as follows:

NONE
LITTLE experience (but not enough, in your judgment)
SUFFICIENT experience for performing your duties
EXTENSIVE experience that goes beyond your present duties

- Your answers will assist in a continuing effort to provide better training.
- Your answers will be handled in the strictest confidence.
- Your answers will be tabulated with those of others to determine training needs, content requirements, and format preferences.
- The questionnaire will present a multilayered offering of skills with which you may or may not be acquainted, so please be candid and thorough in completing it.
- Data collected will be used to design future training classes that you and your fellow employees will receive.

Task/Skill	Experience Level (Check One)			
	None	**Little**	**Sufficient**	**Extensive**
Selected Skills				
Turn on the computer	☐	☐	☐	☐
Insert and remove a floppy disk	☐	☐	☐	☐
Insert and remove a CD-ROM disk	☐	☐	☐	☐
Reboot the computer	☐	☐	☐	☐

Task/Skill	Experience Level (Check One)			
	None	Little	Sufficient	Extensive
File and Disk Activities				
Saving a file	☐	☐	☐	☐
Backing up a file	☐	☐	☐	☐
Using a floppy disk	☐	☐	☐	☐
Copying a disk	☐	☐	☐	☐
Downloading	☐	☐	☐	☐
Identification Skills				
Identify floppy drive	☐	☐	☐	☐
Identify CD-ROM	☐	☐	☐	☐
Identify monitor	☐	☐	☐	☐
Identify printer	☐	☐	☐	☐
Identify internal modem	☐	☐	☐	☐
Identify sound card	☐	☐	☐	☐
General Skills				
Identify computer ports (i.e., printer, keyboard, monitor, mouse)	☐	☐	☐	☐
Select items with a mouse pointer	☐	☐	☐	☐
Access Windows features with start button	☐	☐	☐	☐
Open pop-up menus with a mouse	☐	☐	☐	☐
Point at menu item	☐	☐	☐	☐
Select and open menu item	☐	☐	☐	☐
Close menu item	☐	☐	☐	☐
Choose commands by pointing and clicking	☐	☐	☐	☐
Maximize and minimize window	☐	☐	☐	☐
Use horizontal and vertical scroll bars	☐	☐	☐	☐
View contents of floppy disk	☐	☐	☐	☐
View contents of hard disk	☐	☐	☐	☐
View contents of CD-ROM disk	☐	☐	☐	☐
Exit Windows with Shut Down command	☐	☐	☐	☐

Task/Skill	Experience Level (Check One)			
	None	Little	Sufficient	Extensive
Determining Your Software Needs				
Word	☐	☐	☐	☐
Excel	☐	☐	☐	☐
Access	☐	☐	☐	☐
Outlook	☐	☐	☐	☐
PowerPoint	☐	☐	☐	☐
Front Page	☐	☐	☐	☐
Publisher	☐	☐	☐	☐
Accessing the Web				
Launch Web browser	☐	☐	☐	☐
Access a URL	☐	☐	☐	☐
Identify a search engine	☐	☐	☐	☐
Use a search engine	☐	☐	☐	☐
Finding What You Need on the Web				
Perform an advanced search	☐	☐	☐	☐
Search using Boolean expressions	☐	☐	☐	☐
Find an e-mail address	☐	☐	☐	☐
Find a telephone number	☐	☐	☐	☐
Find a street address	☐	☐	☐	☐
Find a picture file	☐	☐	☐	☐
Find a sound file	☐	☐	☐	☐
Find a movie file	☐	☐	☐	☐
Find a streaming video file	☐	☐	☐	☐
Performing Online Interactive Tasks				
Complete/submit an online application	☐	☐	☐	☐
Complete an online survey	☐	☐	☐	☐
Refresh a Web page	☐	☐	☐	☐
Bookmark a Web page	☐	☐	☐	☐
Return to previously viewed Web pages	☐	☐	☐	☐
Print a Web page	☐	☐	☐	☐
Organize "favorites"	☐	☐	☐	☐

Task/Skill	Experience Level (Check One)			
	None	**Little**	**Sufficient**	**Extensive**
Basic browser functions (Forward, Back, Home)	☐	☐	☐	☐
Additional Skills				
Conduct a virus scan (on a floppy disk)	☐	☐	☐	☐
Use a scanning device	☐	☐	☐	☐
E-Mail Utilities				
Establish a free e-mail account	☐	☐	☐	☐
Use Address Book	☐	☐	☐	☐
Compose and send e-mail message	☐	☐	☐	☐
Tack on an attachment to e-mail message	☐	☐	☐	☐

- Are there any technology classes specific to your work that you would suggest adding to the continuing education and training schedule? If so, list them here: _____.
- Would you be interested in taking a technology training course through Web-based training at your desktop rather than attending a live class with other students? (please check one)

  Yes _____

  No _____
- Besides technology training, what **other types** of training classes would you suggest the library offer? (e.g. Customer Service, Stress Management, Crisis Management, Managing Change, Problem Solving, Time Management, etc.) _____

  _____.
- In which location (if multiple locations) would you prefer to receive training? _____
- Job Title _____(optional)

STAFF TRAINING OUTCOMES—SEFLIN EVALUATION SURVEY

- This survey is intended to measure your assessment of the SEFLIN Technology Training Program for Southeast Florida Library Staff.
- Key survey objectives appear in italics above each set of questions so that you can refer to these as you reply.
- The information that you provide will directly impact how SEFLIN plans future technology training, so please respond responsibly and honestly.
- We ask that you return this survey to SEFLIN by [four weeks after distribution].

(Multiple choice questions 1-26)

Part I: Background

1. What is your position? (Check only one answer.)
   __ Administration (Director, Assistant Director, Department/Unit Head)
   __ Public Services (Reference, Circulation, etc.)
   __ Technical Services (Cataloging, Collection Development, etc.)
   __ Other Services (Personnel, Accounting, etc.)

2. Does your position require an MLS degree? (Check only one answer.)
   __ Yes
   __ No

3. What is your library type? (Check only one answer.)
   __ Public
   __ Academic
   __ Special
   __ School

4. How many years have you worked in libraries? (Check only one answer.)
   __ Less than 1 year
   __ 1-5 years
   __ 6-10 years
   __ 11-15 years
   __ 16-20 years
   __ More than 20 years

5. What type of classes/courses have you taken? (Check all categories that apply.)
   __ Dedicated classes held in library technology training labs
   __ Voucher classes held in CompUSA training labs
   __ Web-based ElementK courses delivered online

Part II: Knowledge/Skills in Using Technology

Scale for Answering Questions in Part II

Please select number that applies to each question and write it in next to that question.

Not at all   1
Rarely   2
To a moderate extent   3
To a great extent   4
To a very great extent 5

Use of Technology Knowledge/Skills Before and After Training

___ 6. To what extent did you use technology knowledge/skills *before* taking classes through the SEFLIN technology training program?

___ 7. To what extent are you using technology knowledge/skills *after* taking classes through the SEFLIN technology training program?

Confidence in Ability to Use Technology Knowledge/Skills

___ 8. To what extent has your confidence in using technology increased as a result of the SEFLIN Technology Training Program?

Support and Barriers to Learning

___ 9. To what extent did you receive assistance from your local Library Training Administrator in preparing you for the SEFLIN Technology Training Program?

___10. To what extent have you received help from and/or support of your direct supervisor in applying the technology knowledge/skills learned through the SEFLIN Technology Training Program?

___11. To what extent have you had the time to use the technology knowledge/skills learned through the SEFLIN technology training program?

___12. To what extent have you had access to the necessary resources (e.g., equipment and information) to apply the technology knowledge/skills learned in the SEFLIN technology training program?

Learning Impact Measures

___13. To what extent has the content of courses you have taken through the SEFLIN Technology Training Program accurately reflected the technology knowledge/skills needed on your job?

___14. To what extent has the SEFLIN Technology Training Program improved your *daily* performance on the job?

___15. To what extent has the SEFLIN Technology Training Program improved your *overall* job performance?

Part III: Program Design and Delivery

Scale for Answering Questions in Part III

Please select number that applies to each question and write it in next to that question. (Note the different rating indicators in this scale.)

Strongly Disagree	1
Disagree	2
Neither	3
Agree	4
Strongly Agree	5

Effectiveness of Delivery Methods

___16. Dedicated classes held in library technology training labs are an effective way to learn.

___17. Voucher classes held in CompUSA training labs are an effective way to learn.

___18. Web-based ElementK courses delivered online are an effective way to learn.

___19. Training facilities and equipment were favorable to learning:
At library technology training labs
At CompUSA training labs
At your local library job site
At your home

___ 20. I was able to take technology classes/courses at a time and place convenient for my schedule.

Content

___ 21. I had the information needed to start each class/course.

___ 22. I clearly understood class/course objectives.

___ 23. Classes/courses met all stated objectives.

__ 24. If you have taken dedicated or voucher classes:
Materials provided were useful
I had enough time to learn the subject matter
Course/class content was logically organized
Help was available when I needed assistance

__ 25. If you have taken Web-based courses online through ElementK:
Materials provided were useful
I had enough time to learn the subject matter
Course/class content was logically organized
Help was available when I needed assistance

Rating of Program Design and Delivery

26. How would you rate the overall program design and delivery of the SEFLIN Technology Training Program? (Check only one answer.)
__ Excellent
__ Good
__ Average
__ Below Average
__ Failure

(Open-ended questions 27-30)

Improving Program Design and Delivery

27. What is your single most important recommendation for improving the *quality of instruction* in the SEFLIN Technology Training Program?

28. What are your specific or general recommendations for making the SEFLIN Technology Training Program better address your needs?

Part IV: Impact of Learned Knowledge/Skills on Library Users

29. The ultimate goal of the SEFLIN Technology Training Program is to improve library services for library users. Do you have a specific experience you can share on how a library user(s) has been better served or a library service improved due to your new technology knowledge/skills? Please share as much detail as appropriate. If you prefer, please attach your written story to the survey.

30. Other comments . . .

Notes

Chapter 1

1. American Library Association. "Library Support Staff Interests Round Table," April 3, 2002. Available at <http://www.ala.org/ssirt>.

Chapter 2

1. American Library Association. "What is UCITA?" November 27, 2001. Available at <http://www.ala.org/washoff/ucita/what.html>.

Chapter 3

1. Godbout, Alain J. "Managing Core Competencies: The Impact of Knowledge Management on Human Resources Practices in Leading Edge Organizations." Document Technique, 1998: No. 98, p. 88.
2. University of California, Riverside—Human Resources Department. "UCR Guide to Core Competencies Program," February 15, 2002. Available at <http://humanresources.ucr.edu/HRUnits/Competency/GuidetoCompetencies.html>.
3. Ibid.
4. Ibid.
5. New Jersey Library Association. NJLA Professional Development Committee Core Competencies Ad Hoc Committee. "Core Competencies for Librarians," October 19, 1999. Available at <http://www.njla.org/statements/competencies.html>.
6. Ibid.
7. California Library Association. "Competencies for California Librarians in the 21st Century," December 16, 1999. Available at <http://cla-net.org/pubs/Competencies.html>.
8. Ibid.
9. Tampa Bay Library Consortium. Design Committee. "Core Competencies," September 21, 2001. Available at <http://www.tblc.org>.
10. Mcfail, Mairi. "Technology Competencies for Library Staff," Fall 1998. Oakland Public Library. Modified April 12, 2002.
11. UCR—HRD.

Chapter 5

1. Van Buren, Mark. *State of the Industry.* (Report 2002). Alexandria, VA: ASTD, February 2002.

Chapter 7

1. *Buildings, Books and Bytes: Libraries and Communities in the Digital Age.*
Washington, DC: Benton Foundation, 1996. Available at <http://www.benton.org/
Library/Kellogg/summary.html>.
2. Fox, Bette-Lee. "Keep on Constructin'." Library Journal, December 2001,
p. 48.

Chapter 8

1. Lougee, Wendy Pratt. "Perspectives on the Future of Virtual Libraries."
SOLINET Conference on Virtual Libraries in the New Millenium, Atlanta, GA,
May 2001. Available at <http://www-personal.umich.edu/~wlougee/>.
2. Green, David G., R. Eddy, and P. Brist. "Virtual Libraries," Environmental and
Information Sciences, Charles Sturt University Albury New South Wales, Australia,
1999. Available at <http://life.csu.edu.au/gis/finland/sin/>.
3. Ackermann, Ernest. "Directories and Virtual Libraries." Franklin, Beedle,
and Associates, Incorporated, Wilsonville, OR, 2000. Available at <http://www.
webliminal.com/search/search-web04.html#>.
4. Santa Fe Planning Workshop on Distributed Knowledge Work Environments:
Digital Libraries. (Report, 1997) (March 9-11, 1997). Available at <www.dlib.org/
dlib/october97/10editorial.html>.
5. Lougee. "Perspectives on the Future of Virtual Libraries."
6. Caplan, Priscilla. "The Virtual Library: Progress to Date." 2001 SOLINET
Annual Meeting Preconference: "Virtual Libraries in the New Millenium," Atlanta,
Georgia, May 2, 2001. Available at <www.solinet.net/presvtn/vl/ vlibraries.htm>.
7. Rogers, Michael. "WebFeat Offers Simultaneous Search of OPAC/Data-
bases." *Library Journal,* April 1, 2001, p. 27.

Chapter 9

1. Hirshon, Arnold. "Consortia Speaking." *The Journal of Academic Librarianship,* 27(2): 149-151, 2000.

Chapter 10

1. The Institute of Museum and Library Services. "Who We Are." Washington,
DC, 2002. Available at <http://www.imls.gov/about/index.htm>.
2. National Endowment for the Humanities. "Who We Are." Washington, DC
2002. Available at <http://www.neh.gov/whoweare/index.html>.
3. American Library Association. "ALA Launches LSTA Web Page, Brochure."
Chicago: ALA, October 18, 2001. Available at <http://www.ala.org/washoff/lsta.
html>.

Bibliography:
A Practical Resource
for the Library Manager

For the new library manager, the presence of readily accessible resources to help him or her avoid reinventing the wheel with the creation and implementation of each new program will prove invaluable. Since libraries are only recently beginning to use market research prior to the installation of a new program or service rather than simply analyzing success or failure after the program has been established, it is increasingly important for the library manager to be aware of the many resources available. I cannot stress too highly the importance of evaluating a potential program or service prior to its implementation. Libraries no longer have the luxury of starting a program and assuming it will be funded year after year without measurable success.

These bibliographies include print and electronic sources. They cover a number of topics discussed in this text, and they support the text in that the items included are invaluable for understanding the major issues facing today's library manager.

A Selected General Bibliography

Books

Barclay, Donald, ed. *Teaching Electronic Information Literacy.* New York: Neal-Schuman Publishers, 1995.

Beck, Sara Ramser. *Library Training for Staff and Customers.* New York: Haworth Information Press, 1999.

Belasco, James A. *Teaching the Elephant to Dance: Empowering Change in Your Corporation.* New York: Crown, 1990.

Belcastro, Patricia. *Evaluating Library Staff.* Chicago: ALA Editions, 1998.

Bertot, John Carlo, McClure, Charles R., and Ryan, Joe. *Statistics and Performance Measures for Public Library Networked Services.* Chicago: American Library Association, 2000.

Bessler, Joanne M. *Putting Service into Library Staff Training.* Chicago: ALA Editions, 1994.

Blanchard, D. Kenneth, Johnson, Spencer, and Blanchard, Kenneth H. *The One Minute Manager.* New York: Berkley Books, 1982.

Blanchard, Kenneth H., Carlos, John, Randolph, Alan, and Blanchard, Ken. *The 3 Keys to Empowerment: Release the Power Within People for Astonishing Results.* San Francisco: Berrett-Uoehler Publishers, 1999.

Brophy, Peter, Coulling, Kate, ASLIB. *Quality Management for Information and Library Managers.* Aldershot, UK: Gower Pub. Co., 1996.

Bruwelheide, Janis H. *Copyright Primer for Librarians and Educators.* Chicago: ALA Editions, 1995.

Burgstahlwer, Sheryl, Comden, Dan, and Fraser, Beth. *Universal Access.* Chicago: ALA Editions, 1998.

Burlingame, Dwight, ed. *Library Fundraising.* Chicago: ALA Editions, 1995.

Cargill, Jennifer and Webb, Gisela M. *Managing Libraries in Transition.* Phoenix: Oryx Press, 1988.

Carson, Kerry David and Carson, Paula Phillips. *Library Manager's Deskbook.* Chicago: ALA Editions, 1995.

Carson, Kerry David, Carson, Paula Phillips, and Phillips, Joyce Schouest. *The ABCs of Collaborative Change: The Manager's Guide to Library Renewal.* Chicago: ALA Editions, 1997.

Childers, Thomas and Van House, Nancy. *What's Good?* Chicago: ALA Editions, 1998.

Corson-Finnerty, Adam and Blanchard, Laura. *Fundraising and Friend-Raising on the Web.* Chicago: ALA Editions, 1998.

Coyle, Karen. *Coyle's Information Highway Handbook.* Chicago: ALA Editions, 1997.

Crawford, Walt and Gorman, Michael. *Future Libraries.* Chicago: ALA Editions, 1995.

Crews, Kenneth D. *Copyright Essentials for Librarians and Educators.* Chicago: ALA Editions, 2000.

Daubert, Madeline J. *Financial Management for Small and Medium-Sized Libraries.* Chicago: ALA Editions, 1993.

Drucker, Peter Ferdinand. *The Frontiers of Management: Where Tomorrow's Decisions Are Being Shaped Today.* New York: Truman Talley Books/Plume, 1999.

Eberhart, George, comp. *Whole Library Handbook 3.* Chicago: ALA Editions, 2000.

Foundation Center, The. *The Foundation Center Guide to Proposal Writing* (Revised Edition). New York: The Foundation Center, 1997.

Foundation Center, The. *The Foundation Center's Guide to Grantseeking on the Web.* New York: The Foundation Center, 1998.

Foundation Center, The. *Foundation Fundamentals* (Sixth Edition). New York: The Foundation Center, 1999.

Foundation Center, The. *Libraries and Information Services (Grant Guide).* New York: The Foundation Center, 1999.

Foundation Center, The. *Literacy, Reading and Adult/Continuing Education (Grant Guide).* New York: The Foundation Center, 1999.

Foundation Center, The. *National Guide to Funding for Information Technology.* New York: The Foundation Center, 1999.

Foundation Center, The. *National Guide to Funding for Libraries and Information Services* (Fifth Edition). New York: The Foundation Center, 1999.

Gertzog, Alice. *Administration of the Public Library*. Lanham, MD: Scarecrow Press, 1994.

Giesecke, Joan, ed. *The Dynamic Library Organizations in a Changing Environment*. Binghamton: Haworth Press, 1995.

Giesecke, Joan, ed. *Practical Help for New Supervisors*. Chicago: ALA Editions, 1996.

Giesecke, Joan, ed. *Scenario Planning for Libraries*. Chicago: ALA Editions, 1998.

Goleman, Daniel P. *Emotional Intelligence*. New York: Bantam Books, 1995.

Hafner, Arthur W. *Descriptive Statistical Techniques for Librarians*. Chicago: ALA Editions, 1998.

Hannah, Stan A. and Harris, Michael H. *Inventing the Future: Information Services for a New Millennium*. Connecticut: Ablex Publishing, 2000.

Hardy, Cynthia. *Power and Politics in Organizations*. Hampshire, U.K.: Dartmouth Pub. Co., 1995.

Haricombe, Lorraine J. and Lucher, T.J., eds. *Creating the Agile Library*. Westport, CT: Greenwood Publishing Group, 1998.

Hartsook, Robert. *Closing That Gift!* Wichita: ASR Philanthropic Publishing, 1998.

Hartsook, Robert. *How to Get Million Dollar Gifts and Have Donors Thank You: 101 Strategies Every Fund Raiser Should Know*. Wichita: ASR Philanthropic Publishing, 1999.

Hayes, Robert M. and Walter, Virginia. *Strategic Management for Public Libraries*. Westport, CT: Greenwood Publishing Group, 1996.

Hernon, Peter and Altman, Ellen. *Assessing Service Quality*. Chicago: ALA Editions, 1998.

Hernon, Peter and Whitman, John R. *Delivering Satisfaction and Service Quality: A Customer-Based Approach for Libraries*. Chicago: American Library Association, 2000.

Hollands, William D. *Teaching the Internet to Library Staff and Users: 10 Ready-to-Go Workshops That Work*. New York and London: Neal-Schuman Publishers, 1999.

I Ching (Book of Changes). Princeton: Princeton University Press, 1967.

Jones, Barbara M. *Libraries, Access and Intellectual Freedom*. Chicago: ALA Editions, 1999.

Kahn, Miriam B. *Disaster Planning for Libraries*. Chicago: ALA Editions, 1998.

Karp, Rashelle S., ed. *Part-Time Public Relations with Full-Time Results*. Chicago: ALA Editions, 1995.

Kelly, James N. and Gouillart, Francis. *Transforming the Organization*. New York: McGraw-Hill, 1995.

Kenney, Lisa F. *Lobby for Your Library*. Chicago: ALA Editions, 1992.

Martin, Murray S. and Wolf, Martin T. *Budgeting for Information Access*. Chicago: ALA Editions, 1998.

Mason, Marilyn Gell. *Strategic Management for Today's Libraries.* Chicago: ALA Editions, 1999.

Mayo, Diane and Nelson, Sandra. *Wired for the Future.* Chicago: ALA Editions, 1998.

McCabe, Gerard. *Planning for a New Generation of Public Library Buildings.* Westport, CT: Greenwood Press, 2000.

Miller, Glenn. *Customer Service and Innovation in Libraries.* Fort Atkinson, WI: Highsmith Co., 1996.

Nelson, Sandra, Altman, Ellen, and Mayo, Diane. *Managing for Results.* Chicago: ALA Editions, 1999.

Office of Intellectual Freedom. *Intellectual Freedom Manual.* Chicago: ALA Editions, 1996.

Peck, Robert S. *Libraries, the First Amendment, and Cyberspace: What You Need to Know.* Chicago: ALA Editions, 1999.

Peters, Thomas J. and Waterman, Robert H. Jr. *In Search of Excellence.* New York: Harper & Row, 1982.

Peters, Tom. *Thriving on Chaos: Handbook for a Management Revolution.* New York: Alfred A. Knopf, 1988.

Peters, Tom, Austin, Nancy C., and Peters, Thomas J. *A Passion for Excellence: The Leadership Difference.* New York, Warner Books, 1985.

Raitt, David I. *Libraries for the New Millennium: Implications for Managers.* Lanham, MD: Bernan Associates, 1997.

Reed, Sally Gardner. *Saving Your Library: A Guide to Getting, Using and Keeping the Power You Need.* Jefferson, NC: McFarland and Company, 1992.

Rounds, Richard S. *Basic Budgeting Practices for Librarians.* Chicago: ALA Editions, 1994.

Rubin, Renee. *Avoiding Liability Risk.* Chicago: ALA Editions, 1994.

Senge, Peter M. *The Fifth Discipline.* New York: Doubleday/Currency, 1990.

Sheldon, Brooke E. *Leaders in Libraries.* Chicago: ALA Editions, 1991.

Shonrock, Diana, ed. *Evaluating Library Instruction.* Chicago: ALA Editions, 1995.

Shuman, Bruce A. *Library Security and Safety Handbook.* Chicago: ALA Editions, 1999.

Slusar, Linda, College of Dupage, Johnson, Debra Wilcox. *Soaring to Excellence: Techno-Lust, Techno-Stress and Techno-Babble.* Chicago: ALA Editions, 2000.

Slusar, Linda, College of Dupage, Brandt, D. Scott. *Soaring to Excellence: Tools of the Trade III.* Chicago: ALA Editions, 2000.

Smith, G. Stevenson. *Accounting for Libraries and Other Not-for-Profit Organizations.* Chicago: ALA Editions, 1999.

Steele, Victoria and Elder, Stephen D. *Becoming a Fundraiser.* Chicago: ALA Editions, 1992.

Stephens, Annabel K. *Assessing the Public Library Planning Process.* Stamford, CT: Ablex Pub. Corp., 1995.

Stover, Mark. *Leading the Wired Organization: The Information Professional's Guide to Managing Technological Change.* New York: Neal Schuman, 1999.

Stueart, Robert D. *Library Management.* Englewood, NJ: Libraries Unlimited, 1993.

Sutton, Dave. *So You're Going to Run a Library: A Library Management Primer.* Englewood: Libraries Unlimited, 1995.

Symons, Ann K. and Reed, Sally Gardner. *Speaking Out!* Chicago: ALA Editions, 1999.

The Taft Group (for ALA). *Big Book of Library Grant Money.* Chicago: ALA Editions, 1998.

Townsend, Robert. *Further Up the Organization.* New York: Alfred A. Knopf, 1984.

Ware, James, Gebauer, Judith, Hartman, Amir, and Roldan, Malu. *The Search for Digital Excellence.* New York: McGraw Hill, 1997.

Weingand, Darlene. *Administration of the Small Public Library.* Chicago: ALA Editions, 1992.

Weingand, Darlene. *Customer Service Excellence.* Chicago: ALA Editions, 1997.

Weingand, Darlene. *Future-Driven Library Marketing.* Chicago: ALA Editions, 1997.

Weingand, Darlene. *Managing Today's Public Library.* Englewood, NJ: Libraries Unlimited, 1994.

Williams, Delmus E. and Garten, Edward D., eds. *Advances in Library Administration and Organization: 1999* (Vol.16). Stanford, CA: JAI Press, 1999.

Wilson, Lucille. *People Skills for Library Managers: A Common Sense Guide for Beginners.* Englewood, NJ: Libraries Unlimited, 1996.

Wilson, William James and Himmel, Ethel. *Planning for Results: A Public Library Transformation Process.* Chicago: ALA Editions, 1998.

A Selected Bibliography on Career Planning in Libraries

Articles

Burns, Taodhg. "New World of Information Professionalism." *Information Outlook,* 3(7), 1999: 25-29.

Church, Doug. "Breaking Free of the Reference Shackles." *Information Outlook,* 3(3), 1999: 18-20.

Church, Doug. "Ch-Ch-Changes: What Does the Future Hold for Information Professionals?" *Information Outlook,* 4(5), 2000: 20-24.

Corcoran, Mary. "Industry Insights: Changing Roles of Information Professionals: Choices and Implications." *Online,* 24(2), 2000: 72-74.

Corcoran, Mary, Lynn Dagar, and Anthea Stratigos. "The Changing Roles of Information Professionals: Excerpts from an Outsell, Inc. Study." *Online,* 24(2), 2000: 28-34.

Crosby, John. "Claim Your Territory." *Workplace Libraries '99,* 2(June), 1999: 1.

Dolan, Donna R. and John Schumacher. "New Jobs Emerging in and Around Libraries and Leadership." *Online,* 21(6), 1997: 68-76.

Douglas, Gretchen V. "Professor Librarian: A Model of the Teaching Librarian of the Future." *Computers in Libraries,* 19(10), 1999: 24-30.

Duberman, Josh. "Reflections in a Fun House Mirror: Web Trends and Evolving Roles for Information Specialists." *Searcher,* 7(2), 1999: 30.

Easun, Susan, ed. "The Roles of Professionals, Paraprofessionals and Nonprofessionals: A View from the Academy." *Library Trends,* 46(3), 1998: 426-596.

Evensky, Harold. "I'd Rather Be a Librarian." *Financial Planning,* January 1999: 168.

Fichter, Darlene. "Intranet Librarian—Search Master: A New Role for Information Professionals." *Online,* 24(2), 2000: 76-78.

Francois, Valerie Gray. "Librarians Take the Spotlight." *National Business Employment Weekly,* September 26-October 2, 1999: 25, 28.

Hohhof, Bonnie and Lera Chitwood. "At a Crossroads: Information Professional to Intelligence Analyst." *Information Outlook,* 4(2), 2000: 20-25.

Katz-Stone, Adam. "Web Overturning Image of Book-Filing Librarian." *Washington Business Journal,* April 3, 2000.

Kuhlthau, Carol Collier. "The Role of Experience in the Information Search Process of an Early Career Information Worker: Perceptions of Uncertainty, Complexity, Construction and Sources." *Journal of the American Society for Information Science,* 50(5), 1999: 399-412.

Latharn, Joyce. "The World Online: IT Skills for the Practical Professional." *American Libraries,* 31(3), 2000: 40-42.

Lettis, Lucy. "Are We Keeping Pace With Change?" *Information Outlook,* 3(3), 1999: 24-26.

Lettis, Lucy. "The Future of Information Professionals: Seize the Day." *Information Outlook,* 4(5), 2000: 26-32.

Mangan, Katherine. "In Revamped Library Schools Information Trumps Books: Institution's New Curricula and New Names Reflect Student Interests and the Job Market." *The Chronicle of Higher Education,* 46(31), 2000.

Ojala, Marydee. "What Will They Call Us in the Future?" *Special Libraries,* 84(4), 1993: 226-229.

Pack, Thomas. "The Changing Role of the Information Vendor." *Online,* 24(2), 2000: 36-40.

Pantry, Sheila. "Whither the Information Profession? Challenges and Opportunities: The Cultivation of Information Professionals for the New Millenium." *Aslib Proceedings,* 49(6), 1997: 170-172.

Paris, Marion. "Beyond Competencies: A Trendspotter's Guide to Library Education." *Information Outlook,* 3(12), 1999: 31-36.

Reinke, Janet. "Should Librarians Have the MLS Degree?" *Library Journal,* 122(12), 1997: 12-13.

Rurak, Maura. "Technology Sparks Demand for Cyber-Librarians." *National Business Employment Weekly,* February 16-22, 1997: 25-26.

Rutherford, LeAne. "Taking Charge of Your Professional Life: A Special Librarian's Guide to Greater Work Satisfaction." *Information Outlook,* September 1999: 17-22.

Smythe, David. "Facing the Future: Preparing New Information Professionals." *The Information Management Journal,* 33(2), 1999: 44-48.

St. Clair, Guy. "Qualification Management in Information Services: MX Grand Design." *Information Outlook,* 4(6), 2000: 32-36.

Strateigos, Anthea. "Industry Insights: Choose Your Future." *Online,* 24(1), 2000: 64-66.

Tenopir, Carol. "I Never Learned About That in Library School: Curriculum Changes in LIS." *Online,* 24(2), 2000: 43-46.

U.S. Dept. of Labor. "New Occupations Emerging Across Industry Lines." *Issues in Labor Statistics,* Summary 98-110, November 1998.

Watkins, Christine. "Can Librarians Play Basketball?" *American Libraries,* 30(3), 1999: 58-61.

White, Herbert S. "Where Is the Profession Heading?" *Library Journal,* 124(19), 1999: 44-45.

Youngman, Daryl C. "Library Staffing Considerations in the Age of Technology: Basic Elements for Managing Change." *Issues in Science and Technology Librarianship,* Fall 1999. Available at <http://www.library.ucsb.edu/istl/99-fall/articles.html>.

Books

Rehman, Sajjad ur. *Preparing the Information Professional: An Agenda for the Future.* Westport, CT: Greenwood Press, 2000.

A Selected Bibliography on Core Competencies

Articles

Mouer, Susan. "The Australian Library Industry Competency Standards: Present Perspectives and Future Prospects." *The Australian Library Journal,* 46(2), 1997: 136-146.

Paris, Marion. "Beyond Competencies: A Trendspotter's Guide to Library Education." *Information Outlook,* 3(12), 1999: 31-36.

Stambaugh, Laine. "Academic Libraries: Are Your Library Support Staff Classifications Ready for the Twenty-First Century." *Library Administration and Management,* 14(3), 2000: 167-171.

Books

Spiegelman, Barbara. *Competencies for Special Librarians of the 21st Century.* Washington, DC: SLA, 1997.

Web Sites

http://cla-net.org/pubs/Competencies.html
http://humanresources.ucr.edu
www.apl.org/policies/tecplan.html
www.contactcentre.com.au/core_competencies.htm
www.farmingdale.edu/CampusPages/ComputingAndLibrary/Library/corecomp.html
www.infotoday.com/cilmag/jan98/story2.htm
www.mnpl.org/core
www.oaklandlibrary.org/techcomp.htm
www.ravenworks.com/leadership/core_competencies.htm
www.riarlington.com/corecomp.html
www.solonline.org

A Selected Bibliography on the Issue of Training and Development

The following are available exclusively from The American Society for Training and Development (ASTD Press, 1640 King Street, Box 1443, Alexandria, VA. 22313-2043, Tel. 800-628-2783, Fax 703-683-8103, <www.astd.org>.

Alden, Jay. *A Trainer's Guide to Web-Based Instruction.*
Bonner, Dede, ed. *In Action: Leading Knowledge Management and Learning.*
Broad, Mary L., ed. *In Action: Transferring Learning to the Workplace.*
Cherniss, Cary and Adler, Mitchel. *Promoting Emotional Intelligence in Organizations.*
Driscoll, Margaret. *Web Based Training.*
Ellis, Alan L., Longmire, Warren R., and Wagner, Ellen D. *Managing Web-Based Training.*
Gupta, Kavita. *A Practical Guide to Needs Assessment.*
Hale, Judith. *The Performance Consultant's Field-Book.*
Harrison, Nigel. *How to Design Self-Directed and Distance Learning Programs.*
Head, Glenn. *Training Cost Analysis.*
Kirkpatrick, Donald, ed. *Another Look at Evaluating Training.*
Lawson, Karen. *Improving On-the-Job Training and Coaching.*
Mantyla, Karen. *Interactive Distance Learning Exercises That Really Work!*
Mantyla, Karen and Gividen, J. Richard. *Distance Learning: A Step-by-Step Guide for Trainers.*
Marx, Raymond J. *ASTD Media Selection Tool for Workplace Learning.*
McArdle, Geri E. *Training Design and Delivery.*
McCain, Donald V. *Creating Training Courses.*
Phillips, Jack J., ed. *In Action: Measuring Return-on-Investment,* Vol. 2.

Phillips, Jack J. *Return-on-Investment in Training and Performance Improvement Programs.*

Robinson, Dana Gaines and Robinson, James C., eds. *Moving from Training to Performance.*

Robinson, Dana Gaines and Robinson, James C. *Performance Consulting.*

Rothwell, William J. *ASTD Models for Human Performance.*

Rothwell, William J. *ASTD Models for Workplace Learning and Performance.*

Scott, Beverly. *Consulting on the Inside.*

Web Sites

http://cted.inel.gov/cted
www.astd.org
www.filename.com/wbt/_private/resources.htm
www.flash.net/~gizmo/hcode/training.htm
www.ittrain.com/guide/guide-index-product.html
www.masie.com/trlinks.htm
www.multimediatraining.com/links.html
www.qualitymag.com/trainingresources.html
www.tcm.com/trdev
www.techsoup.org
www.trainingnet.com
www.trainingsupersite.com
www.trainnet.com
www.wisc.edu/learntech/grp/id.htm
www.zigonperf.com/links.htm

Periodicals

Adult Education Quarterly and *Adult Learning,* American Association for Adult and Continuing Education, 1200 19th Street NW, Suite 300, Washington, DC 20036-2401

Creative Training Techniques Newsletter, Lakewood Publications, 50 S. Ninth Street, Minneapolis, MN 55402

Educational Technology, 700 Palisade Avenue, Englewood Cliffs, NJ 07632

Educom Review, Inter University Communications Council, Inc., 1112 16th Street NW, Suite 600, Washington, DC 20036

The Eric File, ERIC Clearinghouse on Adult, Career and Vocational Education, Center on Education and Training for Employment, Ohio State University, 1900 Kenny Road, Columbus, OH 43210-1090

Evaluation Practice, American Evaluation Association, 401 E. Jefferson St., Suite 205, Rockville, MD 20850

HR Magazine, Society for Human Resource Management, 606 North Washington Street, Alexandria, VA 22314-1997

Inside Technology Training, 9420 Bunsen Parkway, Louisville, KY 40220

International Journal of Training and Development, Blackwell Publishers, P.O. Box 805, 108 Cowley Road, Oxford OK4 1FH, United Kingdom

IT Training, Training Information Network, Ltd., Jubilee House, The Oaks, Ruislip, Middlesex HA4 7LF, United Kingdom

Learning Curve, 5 Speen Street, Framingham, MA 01701

Online Learning, 50 S. Ninth Street, Minneapolis, MN 55402

Performance Improvement, International Society for Performance Improvement, 1300 L. Street NW, Suite 1250, Washington, DC 20005

Training and Development, ASTD, 1640 King Street, Box 1443, Alexandria, VA 22313

Training Magazine, 50 S. Ninth Street, Minneapolis, MN 55402

Workforce Magazine, 245 Fischer Avenue, B-2, Costa Mesa, CA 92626

A Selected Bibliography on Internet Censoring and Filtering

A number of books either concentrate wholly on Internet censoring or include a discussion of these issues as a portion of a larger essay. However, since these issues are so fluid and changes are occurring constantly, it is preferable to recommend a number of online bibliographic resources that concentrate on the issues in a specific and timely manner.

Two reports that are absolutely critical for library managers to become familiar with concentrate on these issues while uncovering and reporting a number of fascinating findings. These are "Public Libraries and the Internet 2000: Summary Findings and Data Tables" by John Carlo Bertot and Charles R. McClure (http://www.nclis.gov/statsurv/2000plo.pdf) and "Survey of Internet Access Management in Public Libraries" by The Library Research Center Graduate School of Library and Information Science, University of Illinois (http://www.lis.uiuc.edu/gslis/research/internet.pdf).

Selected Web List

<http://internet.ggu.edu/university_library/if/>, Site to find most current legal information and related sites (searchable).

<http://www.ala.org/alaorg/oif/filtersandfiltering.html>, Excellent ALA megasite focusing on filters and filtering, Internet legislation, intellectual freedom, the First Amendment, etc.

<http://www.bluehighways.com/tifap>, Site for report on filtering products and their assessments by librarians.

<http://www.cdt.org/>, The site for the Center for Democracy and Technology.

<http://www.copacommission.org/report>, Contains final report of COPA.

<http://www.dpi.state.wi.us/dlcl/pld/netissue.html>, Site presenting issues in public library Internet access.

<http://www.eff.org>, Site of the Electronic Frontier Foundation working to protect privacy, access to online resources, etc.

<http://www.GetNetWise.org/>, Site for families new to the Internet.

<http://www.llrx.com/congress/011599.htm>, Comprehensive site explaining the Child Online Protection Act (COPA) and related information.
<http://www.monroe.lib.in.us/~lchampel/netadv4.html>, Web-based resource guide providing youth access to the Internet.
<http://www.peacefire.org>, Also offers critiques of filtering software.
<http://www.safekids.com>, Concentrates on child safety on the Internet through many links and resources.
<http://www.ssrn.com/update/lsn/cyberspace/csl_menu.html>, Comprehensive site explaining the latest cyberspace laws.

A Selected Bibliography on the Virtual (Digital) Library

Articles

Cleveland, G. "Digital Libraries: Definitions, Issues and Challenges." *UDT Occasional Paper No. 8,3* <http://www.ifla.org/VI/5/op/udtop8/udtop8.htm>.

Coffman, Steve and Susan McGlamery. "The Librarian and Mr. Jeeves." *American Libraries,* 31(5), 2000: 66-69.

Council on Library Resources "Digital Libraries: Dream or Delusion?" <http://www.clir.org/diglib/forums/fall00/forumsum.htm>.

"Digital Collections." <http://www.clir.org/diglib/collections.htm>.

Feldman, Susan. "Digital Libraries '99." *Information Today,* 16(9), 1999: 1-4.

Himmelfarb, Gertrude. "Revolution in the Library." *Library Trends,* 47(4), 1999: 612-620.

Janes, Joseph, David Carter, and Patricia Memmott. "Digital Reference Services in Academic Libraries." *Reference and User Services Quarterly,* 39(2), 1999: 145-150.

Kasowitz, Abby, Blyth Bennett, and R. David Lankes. "Quality Standards for Digital Reference Consortia." *Reference and User Services Quarterly* 39(4), 2000: 355-363.

Lagace, Nettie and Michael McClennen. "Questions and Quirks: Managing an Internet-Based Distributed Reference Service." *Computers in Libraries,* 18(2), 1998: 51-53.

Lankes, David R. "Birth Cries of Digital Reference: An Introduction to This Special Issue." *Reference and User Service Quarterly,* 39(4), 2000: 352-354.

Lynch, Clifford. "Today and Tomorrow: What the Digital Library Really Means for Collections and Services." In *Virtually Yours.* Chicago: ALA Editions, 1999.

Massey-Burzio, Virginia. "The Rush to Technology," *Library Trends,* 47(4), 1999: 620-640.

"Overview of the California Digital Library." <http://www.cdlib.org/about/overview>.

Saunders, Laverna M. "The Human Element in the Virtual Library." *Library Trends,* (47)4, 1999: 771-788.

Schwartz, Candy. "Digital Libraries: An Overview." *The Journal of Academic Librarianship,* 26(6), 2000: 385-393.

Tenopir, Carol. "The Impact of Digital Reference on Librarians and Library Users." *Online,* 22(6), 1998: 84.

Books

Arms, William Y. *Digital Libraries.* Cambridge, MA: MIT Press, 2000.

Janes, Joseph, Lagace, Annette, McKennan, Michael, Carter, David S., Simcox, Schelle, and Ryan, Sara, eds. *The Internet Public Library Handbook.* New York: Neal Schuman, 1999.

Lankes, R. David, Collins, John W., and Kasowitz, Abby S., eds. *Digital Reference Service in the New Millennium.* New York: Neal Schuman, 2000.

Lesk, Michael. *Practical Digital Libraries: Books, Bytes and Bucks.* San Francisco, CA: Morgan Kaufmann, 1997.

Marcum, Deanna B., ed. *Development of Digital Libraries: An American Perspective.* Wesport, CT: Greenwood Press, 2001.

Reingold, Howard. *The Virtual Community: Homesteading on the Electronic Frontier.* New York: HarperPerennial, 1994.

Saunders, Laverna M. *The Virtual Library: Visions and Realities.* Westport, CT: Meckler, 1993.

Stern, David, ed. *Digital Libraries: Philosophies, Technical Design Considerations and Example Scenarios.* Binghamton: Haworth Press, 1999.

Stielow, Frederick, ed. *Creating a Virtual Library: A How-to-Do-It Manual.* New York: Neal Schuman, 1999.

Web Sites

ARL Digital Initiatives Database, <http://www.arl.org/did/>.

Digital Future of Libraries, <http://www.rsl.ru/tacis/manifesto.htm>.

Digital Library Federation, <http://www.clir.org/diglib/dlfhomepage.htm>.

Digital Library Information Resources, <http://sunsite.berkeley.edu/Info/>.

Digital Library Resources, <http://www.canis.uiuc.edu/~bgross/dl/>.

Digital Reference Services: A Bibliography, <http://www.lis.uiuc.edu/~b-sloan/digiref.html>.

D-Lib, <http://www.dlib.org>.

Noerr, Peter. *The Digital Library Toolkit,* second edition, <http://www.sun.com/products-n-solutions/edu/libraries/digitaltoolkit.html>.

Virtual Reference Desk, <http://www.vrd.org>.

E-Journals

D-Lib Magazine, <http://www.dlib.org>.
RLG Diginews, <http://www.rlg.org/preserv/diginews/>.

Index